Mr. Y. Y. Tsu takes
pleasure in presenting
to the ~~C.~~ T. S. Library
Buckley's "Theory &
Practice of Foreign
missions" 1911

Jan 27. 1912

The Nathan Graves Foundation Lectures
delivered before Syracuse University

THEORY AND PRACTICE
OF FOREIGN MISSIONS

BY
JAMES M. BUCKLEY

NEW YORK: EATON & MAINS
CINCINNATI: JENNINGS & GRAHAM

CONTENTS

PAGE

PREFACE... 5

THE FIRST LECTURE
BASIS OF FOREIGN MISSIONS

PHILANTHROPY..................................... 11

RECOMPENSE....................................... 16

THE COMMANDS AND PRAYERS OF THE MASTER........ 18

THE FINAL DOOM OF THE UNCHRISTIANIZED HEATHEN.. 25

"I ALSO WILL SHOW MINE OPINION".............. 29

THE SECOND LECTURE

METHODS, MEANS, AND MEN OF CHRISTIAN MISSIONS

A SURVEY... 41

GENERAL METHODS OF ORGANIZATION................ 43

CONFIRMATION OF THE FOREGOING.................... 47

CONDITIONS OF SUCCESS............................ 55

FINANCIAL PROBLEMS AND PROPERTY TITLES......... 56

VITAL ELEMENTS.................................. 59

THE SELECTION OF MISSIONARIES.................... 61

ELEMENTS OF SUCCESS IN DEALING WITH NON-CHRISTIAN PEOPLES................................. 63

CELIBACY OR MATRIMONY FOR MISSIONARIES.......... 64

SHOULD CONVERTS BE SENT TO CHRISTIAN LANDS FOR EDUCATION FOR THE MINISTRY?.................. 68

SPECIAL MODERN HELPS............................ 70

WORK OF WOMEN'S SOCIETIES...................... 72

CHRIST'S METHOD OF APPROACH NOT OUTWORN...... 74

4   CONTENTS

THE THIRD LECTURE

HINDRANCES AND HELPS TO MISSIONS

PAGE

ELEVEN GRIEVOUS OBSTACLES.................... 83

BUDDHISM...................................... 93

CONFUCIANISM.................................. 94

MOHAMMEDISM.................................. 96

SUBTLE DANGERS IN THE CHRISTIAN CHURCHES........ 102

SEVENTEEN DISTINCT CIRCUMSTANCES FAVORABLE TO
    MISSIONS.................................... 106

THE FOURTH LECTURE

WHAT OF THE PRESENT AND THE FUTURE OF FOREIGN MISSIONS?

PROTESTANT MISSIONS IN ROMAN CATHOLIC COUNTRIES. 121

VALUE OF CORRECT MISSIONARY STATISTICS.......... 125

GRANDEUR OF FOREIGN MISSIONS.................... 126

STRIKING CONTRASTS.............................. 133

MISSIONARY LEADERS............................. 141

THE GIFT OF MISSIONS TO ANTHROPOLOGY............ 147

WHAT OF THE FUTURE?............................ 150

PREFACE

THESE lectures were delivered by the Rev. James Monroe Buckley, D.D., LL.D., before the faculties and students of Syracuse University in the second semester of 1908.

Although they preceded the Edinburgh convention by more than a year, and the program of that convention was not then before the public, it will be seen that Dr. Buckley discussed all of the essential subjects that were before that great body of missionaries and the advocates of the world's missionary movements.

This is not strange, however, as Dr. Buckley had for many years been one of the leaders of missionary thought in his Church, and has been annually a member of the General Missionary Committee, where every part of the missionary world is brought in review and critically considered. No man of this great body has given more intelligent direction to its work or more conscientious and careful study of its methods. By sympathy, by full information, by logical and analytical processes of investigation, Dr. Buckley is an authority upon the subject of Missions. And by full and apt illustration and a lucid and

attractive style he presents the well-worn subject in a way that will engage the attention and
profitably interest the reader.

The lectures of this foundation are delivered
annually at Syracuse University by prominent
authorities upon the great subject of Missions,
now asserting a new and increasing interest in
all Christian Churches.

JAMES R. DAY.

Syracuse University, December 5, 1910.

THE FIRST LECTURE
BASIS OF FOREIGN MISSIONS

THE FIRST LECTURE

BASIS OF FOREIGN MISSIONS

The purpose of the following Lectures was to discuss thoroughly every fundamental principle and method relating to foreign missions, and to point out how they may be best elucidated. As they were to be published subsequent to delivery, they are here presented exactly as read, with the addition of certain extemporaneous explanations and illustrations.

The moral, religious, philanthropic, patriotic, cosmopolitan, and even the pathetic and romantic aspects of Christian Missions would each furnish an inexhaustible supply of inspiring themes for impassioned oratory and writing. Were a Christian waxing old asked to recount his youthful impressions of the missionary movement, he would almost invariably respond that the chief sources of his interest were the display of idols, the graphic recital of the travels and romantic adventures of missionaries, the eloquent appeals, and descriptions of the strange aspect and manners of inhabitants of remote and partially explored regions, their sacred rivers, temples, and sacrificial rites, the Babel-like confusion of tongues, and the shocking tales of martyred missionaries. He would be obliged to state that nothing was more exciting and throng-inspiring than the visits of the few but distinguished missionary secretaries, who combined financial ability and fervent eloquence. They could not, then, present statistics covering almost the whole world, give accounts of great buildings, describe universities, read the records of hospitals vying with those in Christian nations, or emphasize the needs of existing theological institutions.

The subject assumes the existence, truth, and spirit of the Christian religion, and the fact that Missions were begun and are continued by votaries having in view the spread of Christianity and through its means the benefit of mankind. The term "Christian Missions" implies forms of effort put forth in unusual places and among those without the religion of Christ, or those who, bearing the Christian name, have fallen from that faith and practice. The migration of peoples in recent years superinduces upon this generic definition and description missions to those of various religions and languages now domiciled in Christian nations. This condition is partly covered by the term "home missions." Again, the term applies to the unenlightened regions of Christian countries. Their discussion, though as important as any phase of the question, must occupy less space than that of foreign missions, because more is known of one's own country, and because of the peculiar questions which arise in forcing the Christian religion upon countries that have not asked for it, and who boast of religions established ages before the Christian era.

Christian Missions rest upon THREE pillars: Philanthropy, Recompense, and the Commands and Prayers of Christ.

PHILANTHROPY

Philanthropy is such a love of the human race and of the individual man as to generate an intense and constant desire to help others. It does not require the bestowing of all one's substance upon others, but does demand giving to the poor, helping the unfortunate, sympathizing with the sorrowing, and sharing with them the two priceless possessions, knowledge and true religion, possessions which augment in proportion to their distribution.

The best illustration of philanthropy, in the concrete, is the parable of the good Samaritan. The instincts of the Christian heart would naturally prompt to intelligent desire to make known to the whole world the truths and experiences which are the sources of perpetual happiness. The Christian believes that he is in the possession of light and truth, and that where

the Gospel light does not shine, there is error
and darkness. His view includes both the tran-
scendence and the immanence of God; but beyond
the sense of possession of the idea of one Personal
Sovereign God of the universe the sublime doctrine of the Incarnation meets a prime necessity
of human nature. Where it is fully accepted it
at once and forever destroys the needs of idols or
images, gives to the human soul a conception
which transforms it into a temple, in which the
incense of faith continually ascends. The love
of God, as manifested in the gift of Christ, robs
all apparent contradictions, inscrutable phe-
nomena of nature and mysterious Providences
of power to disturb the confidence of man in God,
so that the otherwise distracted spirit can say
within itself: "Though the world be full of
trouble, though my lot be hard, my way ob-
structed, my cry apparently unheeded, hath not
God sent His Son to save me? Then must all
things 'work together for good to me.' "

The offer through Jesus Christ of pardon to
the guilty strikes a blow at bloody sacrifices and
superstitious rites, disintegrates the foundation
of priestcraft, removes the reason for excessive
fasting, flagellation, and all attempts to propi-
tiate God by self-inflicted misery. The realiza-
tion of the sufferings of Christ fills the heart with
such an abhorrence of sin that all the evil conse-

quences which might have followed an uncon-
ditional pardon are more than counteracted, and
the believer is led to consecrate himself to Him
who "died that we may live, who lives that we
may die." Christianity, fully comprehended in
its essentials and firmly believed, undermines the
whole structure of human superstition. The
proverbial saying, "Ignorance is the mother of
devotion," is not true; ignorance is the mother of
superstition.

Christ's life gave to the world its first conception of absolute purity and of a symmetrical
and perfect character. In all ages it has been
observed that particular virtues have been
strongly illustrated in individual lives; but a
perfect character had never before appeared.
Enoch, in the Old Testament, is declared to have
"pleased God," but his life is not described. All
the great characters portrayed in the ancient
books of the Jews were defective or excessive at
certain points—some grievously so. Abraham,
the friend of God; Moses, the inspired legis-
lator; David, as well as Elijah and Elisha, Daniel
and Jeremiah, were obviously imperfect, and one
who should imitate them in every respect would
go widely astray. The inimitable, simple, yet
rigorously analytical portraiture of Christ given
in the four Gospels renders it as valuable to the
world as though the Son of God still walked

among men. Beyond all price is the individualized sympathy of Jesus with the temptations and afflictions of men. His words of love and tenderness to all classes so win the hearts of those who seek the highest that hatred, strife, and all human passions are abashed in His presence. The clear statement of moral principles which the son of Mary and the Son of God gave to the world confers inestimable advantages. Honesty, truth, temperance, chastity, industry, thrift, and the whole catalogue of social virtues are described and prescribed by Christ in a manner to conquer the reason of men of the noblest gifts and secure the mental consent of the humblest peasant.

Before His appearance the Golden Rule was negatively stated; and, perhaps, positively in a few instances, but He placed it in such relation to the love of God as to make it an essential element of the devotion of true worshipers. The unqualified revelation of the duty of forgiveness, the condemnation of pride, arrogance, anger, malice, hatred, and envy—furies that infest the human heart and often deluge the earth with carnage—is peculiar to Christianity.

Various evil passions and deeds had been condemned by philosophers and religious teachers, but the precepts and promises of Christ, more definite and comprehensive, are so related to the needs of man and the worship of God as to impress them upon receptive minds and hearts.

The reciprocal duties of husband and wife, parent and child, master and servant, as laid down in the Gospel, constitute the true foundation of the social fabric. Monogamy is practically a Christian institution. While the Jews received it, they had modified and reversed it by exceptions and divorcement at caprice.

The discrimination, once so prevalent throughout the world and among the ancient Israelites, between male and female offspring, which among various peoples extended to the taking of life, is done away with wherever Christianity prevails, because woman under the Gospel is regarded as man's equal; so that female infanticide is now as heinous a crime as the murder of male infants. How important is Christianity to half the human race will appear from the fact that among the majority of the vast populations of India and China woman is considered far below man, and often treated as though but little above an intelligent beast.

Buddhists, Brahmans, Confucianists, and Mohammedans are amenable to this charge, in varying degrees.

The future life as indicated by Christ includes endless peace, joy, communion with God and all kindred spirits. This inestimable though indescribable boon is placed within the reach of every human being. Only those who willfully refuse the offer of salvation will be denied entrance to the glorious company of the saints.

It is impossible to believe that Christians possessing such spiritual knowledge, joys, and hopes can be indifferent to the pitiable condition of those who have no such teaching, example, promise, and hope.

RECOMPENSE

The history of man reveals no period in which the race was without religion, and as human nature is radically the same in all ages and countries, having like hopes and fears, loves and hatreds, subject to the same depressions, diseases, and death, there will always be religion of some kind. Not one half of the population of the globe are followers of Christ. Christian civilization depends upon the transmission of its possessions to each succeeding generation. Pagan and most other non-Christian religions had been in existence ages before Christianity. Consequently, having the advantage in numbers, they still gain numerically. The failure to recognize this has led some to overestimate the gains of Christianity, and others to underestimate the present rate at which the number of unchristianized people are increasing. Self-protection, therefore, urges Christians to put forth every effort to Christianize the unchristian, and especially the young.

The individual needs of evangelism require the Churches to maintain the internal fires of zeal. Only by imparting can they strengthen inward conviction of spiritual truth and preserve the fervent emotions necessary to support the mind against the tendency to utter absorption in the things which pertain to self-interest. As in Christian lands those professors of the faith not interested in the salvation of their fellows are devoid of the fruits of the Spirit—love, joy, peace, and abounding hope—so a whole denomination living for itself alone will disintegrate for want of propulsive power.

The number and importance of civil, military, and commercial projects continually enlarge, and as they do so Christians should exhibit increasing interest in the grandest of all enterprises, the peaceful conquest of the world by "the sign of the cross." Every congregation of believers is strengthened, elevated, and united by such a conception and its fruits. The protection of our fellow citizens whose business, diplomatic and otherwise, compels them to sojourn in heathen lands, would be sufficient reason for the sending of our missionaries to India, China, Japan, and to the Turkish empire. For the absence of churches in the capitals and large cities of the pagan world would entail much more dissipation, ruin of character, health, and life than does the present situation. The familiar sounds and forms of Christian worship, as has been testified to by many, are a restraining influence upon those who are temporarily or permanently in non-Christian lands. The fever of travel through all lands is increasing with astonishing rapidity, and whole families spend a great proportion of time in restless journeyings—a demoralizing experience unless the facilities for Christian worship be afforded them. Their faith also will be supported by beholding the activity and success of intelligent and spiritually-minded missionaries of their Communions. These are some of the many recompenses for Christians who support foreign missions.

THE COMMANDS AND PRAYERS OF THE MASTER

From the beginning of His ministry Christ claimed the whole world. He declared Himself the Saviour of the world and the Judge of the world; and when He was risen from the dead He spoke unto His apostles, saying: "All power is given unto me in heaven and in earth. *Go* YE therefore, and teach *all nations,* baptizing them in the name of the Father, and of the Son, and of the Holy Ghost; teaching them to observe all things whatsoever I have commanded you: and, lo, I am with you alway, even *unto the end of the world*. Amen." Missions, therefore, are based upon the nature and design of the Gospel.

"The Son of man came to seek and to save that which was lost." He did not give Himself for the salvation of the Jews merely, but for all. "For God so loved the world, that he gave his only begotten Son, that whosoever believeth in him should not perish, but have everlasting life." But the blessings of the Gospel are received by faith, and, being so received, it is necessary to give the materials of faith, which are summed up in the truth.

The much controverted passage in Mark, "Go ye into *all the world* and preach the gospel to every creature," is of the same tenor. It is the commission given to all by the Lord and Master. His command to the apostles has no parallel in history: "And as ye go, *preach,* saying, The kingdom of heaven is at hand. . . . Behold, I send you forth as sheep in the midst of wolves: . . . and ye shall be brought before *governors* and *kings* for my sake, for a testimony against them and the *Gentiles,* . . . and ye shall be hated of all men for my name's sake." "Go ye into all the world" is a commission regardless of race, place, and time. This thought was ever in

Christ's mind, as is shown in Matthew 26. 13:
"Verily I say unto you, Wheresoever *this gospel
shall be preached in the whole world,* there shall
also this, that this woman hath done, be told for a
memorial of her." The injunction applies to all
colors, tongues, and conditions; to the most advanced, who may cavil, and the most degraded,
who may reject. Go: "And as ye go, *preach*"—
as *ambassadors* from your King—the good tidings from Him proclaim authoritatively. It was
a proclamation to kings on their thrones, judges
in their courts, generals at the head of their
armies, philosophers in their schools, prisoners in
their cells, to the rich and to the poor without discrimination. Among all the pronouncements of
this commission none is more impressive and
comprehensive than that in the prayer of Christ,
recorded in the seventeenth chapter of Saint
John, referring to His apostles and those who
already believed on Him: "They are not of the
world, even as I am not of the world. Sanctify
them through thy truth: thy word is truth. As
thou hast sent *me* into *the world,* even so have I
also sent them *into the world.*" "Neither pray I
for these alone, but for *them also which shall be-
live on me* through their word." In all these
passages Christ commits to His followers the
work of establishing His kingdom. Christ spoke
of Himself thus, "I am the light of the world."

And in the Sermon on the Mount He said to His disciples, "Ye are the light of the world." Everywhere the spiritual conquest of the world is the theme of Christ, and all other teaching is subordinate to that purpose.

The disciples, under His instruction, met to receive the promise of Christ: "But ye shall receive power, after that the Holy Ghost is come upon you: and ye shall be witnesses unto me both in Jerusalem and in all Judæa, and in Samaria, and unto the uttermost part of the earth." And to His disciples, as His crucifixion drew near, He said: "And this gospel of the kingdom shall be preached in all the world for a witness unto all nations" (Matthew 24. 14; 28. 19, 20).

Saint Luke records that after the resurrection Christ appeared among His apostles and said: "Thus it is written, and thus it behoved Christ to suffer, and to rise from the dead the third day: and that repentance and remission of sins should be preached in his name among all nations, beginning at Jerusalem" (Luke 24. 46).

Immediately after the day of Pentecost the apostles began to preach to the Jews, and those apostles and brethren who were in Judæa heard that the Gentiles had also received the word of of God; and Peter was put upon his defense. He recounted his vision, and said: "Forasmuch then as God gave them the like gift as he did unto us [the baptism of the Holy Ghost], who believed on the Lord Jesus Christ; what was I, that I could withstand God?" And when the people "heard these things, they held their peace, and glorified God, saying, Then hath God also to the Gentiles granted repentance unto life."

Barnabas and several of the others, including Paul, preached the Gospel to all classes and conditions of men, but not until this circumstance occurred: "When the Jews were gone out of the synagogue, the Gentiles besought that these words might be preached to them the next sabbath. . . . And the next sabbath day came almost the whole city together to hear the word of God." The Jews, angered by the multitudes that followed, denounced this. Peter and John, with unforeseen success, preached the truth to a multitude of Jews from many parts of the world. Yet soon the predictions of Christ were fulfilled. They were thrown into prison; but the number who believed the word was about five thousand. Churches were organized. Then followed the preaching and martyrdom of Stephen.

Peter and the other apostles answered when arrested, "We ought to obey God rather than men"; and, "We are his witnesses of these things." At the conversion of Saint Paul the Lord said to Ananias, "Go thy way: for he is a chosen vessel unto me, to bear my name *before the Gentiles,* and kings, and the children of Israel." From the beginning to the end of the book of Acts the preaching, the journeying from place to place, the conversions, and all other elements of the story can be explained only by the firm conviction that they were commanded by God to preach the Gospel.

It is suggestive to read the traditions of the distribution and work of the other apostles. James is supposed to have remained at Jerusalem; Andrew, to have preached in Scythia, Thrace, Macedonia, Thessaly, and Achaia; Philip, in Upper Asia, Scythia, and Phrygia, where he suffered martyrdom. Bartholomew is said to have penetrated India; Thomas, to have visited Media and Persia, and, possibly, the coast of Coromandel and the island of Ceylon; Matthew, to have gone to Ethiopia, Parthia, and Abyssinia; Simon Zelotes, to Egypt, Cyrenia, Libya, and Mauritania; Jude, to Galilee, Samaria, Idumæa, and Mesopotamia. Saint Paul traveled so extensively, and recorded his experience so minutely, that many countries and cities are identified to this day. On the authority of Sophronius and Theodoret, Saint Paul came across to Britain from Gaul after his second imprisonment. Sophronius was patriarch of Jerusalem in the beginning of the second century; and in a discourse on the merits of the apostles he celebrates Paul's preaching of the Gospel in Spain and Britain. Theodoret was Bishop of Cyprus in the fifth century; and the hypothesis of Paul's visiting Britain is favored by Usher, Parker, Stillingfleet, Camden, and others. In the Epistle to the Romans Saint Paul wrote: "Whensoever I take my journey into Spain I will come to you."

One thing is certain, that during the last sixty years of the first century Christianity was diffused throughout the many countries embraced in the Roman empire, including Egypt, Japan, North Africa, Spain, Gaul, and Britain, and there is no reason to doubt that the Christian Church had, at the least, by the year 100, half a million members besides the large number that had died.

The command of God, and the teachings and labors of the apostles, are indisputable arguments for Missions, and they agree with the other pillars; they make mandatory that which was natural, and are of such a nature that their commanding force will never be diminished.

Were there but one remote island without Christianity, it would be the duty of the Christian world to master its language, and put it in possession of the Pearl of Great Price.

The Final Doom of the Unchristianized Heathen

As countless millions from the beginning, and even at this date, have never heard the sublime story of redemption, the doom of such has been a subject of discussion in all denominations of Christians, and also among doubters of the divine origin of Christianity.

That the heathen would be condemned at the judgment did not conflict with the principles of Augustine and Calvin. The nonelection and consequent reprobation of certain individuals of a ruined race bore the same relation to the stupendous scheme of predestination whether they dwelt in Christian or pagan lands.

The ancient Grecian fathers did not deny the possibility of salvation for the heathen. Justin Martyr and Clement of Alexandria held that the Logos exercised an agency upon the heathen by means of reason, and that heathen philosophers were called, justified, and saved by philosophy. But after the age of Augustine men began to deny the salvation of the heathen, though there were always some who judged more leniently.

Knapp, in his Christian Theology, says:

The truth seems to be this: that none of the heathen will be condemned for not believing in the Gospel, but they are liable to condemnation for the breach of God's natural law; nevertheless, if there be any of them in whom there is a prevailing love to the Divine Being, there seems reason to believe that for the sake of Christ, though to them unknown, they may be accepted by God.

The Presbyterian Confession of Faith contains this passage:

Others not elected, although they may be called by the ministry of the word, and may have some common operations of the Spirit, yet they never truly come to Christ, and therefore cannot be saved; much less can men not professing the Christian religion be saved in any other way whatever, be they never so diligent to frame their lives according to the light of nature and the law of that religion they do profess; and to assert and maintain that they may is very pernicious and to be detested.

As stated by a writer in the Bibliotheca Sacra the belief that all heathen will be punished everlastingly "represents heathen who live according to their light as much less able to be saved than men who hear the Gospel and refuse it; thus directly contradicting our Saviour, who declared that those who rejected His words would receive a heavier condemnation than even the depraved, unrepentant inhabitants of Sodom and Gomorrha, or Tyre and Sidon." "The theory that none of the heathen can be saved dooms the entire population of whole countries to a necessary perdition, with no present hope of pardon; and it extends this judgment backward to generations in the past who are represented as having had no share in that mercy which we have such reason to believe to be universal in its offers. . . . It declares that *there is no possible mercy for the heathen unless Christians choose to carry the Gospel to them,* which practically denies the divine grace by suspending its exercise so far as the heathen, a majority of the human race, are concerned, upon the action of those already enlightened."

Richard Watson says:

The actual state of pagan nations is affectingly bad; but nothing can be deduced from what they are in fact against their salvability; for although there is no ground to hope for the salvation of great numbers of them, actual salvation is one thing, and possible salvation is another. . . . That men were saved under the patriarchal dispensation we know, and at what point, if any, a religion becomes so far corrupted, and truth so far extinct, as to leave no means of salvation to men, nothing to call forth a true faith *in principle*, and obedience to what remains known or knowable of the original law, no one has the right to determine, unless he can adduce some authority from Scripture. . . . We, indeed, know that all are not equally vicious. Nay, that some virtuous heathen have been found in all ages; and some earnest and anxious inquirers after truth, dissatisfied with the notions prevalent in their own countries respectively. . . . But if we knew no such instances of superior virtue and eager desire of religious information among them, the true question . . . would still remain, a question which must be determined not so much by our knowledge of facts which may be very obscure; but such principles and general declarations as we find applicable to the case in the word of God (Theological Institutes of Watson, vol. ii, p. 445).

Dr. Dennis, in Foreign Missions After a Century, writes, "Probation after death is unscriptural and cannot be maintained except by an uncandid, forced, and perilous wresting of the Scriptures." This is incontrovertibly true. But he declares that God has nowhere said that in cases where Christ's mediation is absolutely unrevealed there is no hope of obtaining its benefits. "Who of us would dare to close this door of hope and to decide *ex cathedra* that God was helpless, even though Christ had died and the Spirit lives, to save a soul to whom He had not been pleased to transmit in its fullness the revelation of His redemptive methods?" He, however, says: "We would not advance this message of hope as an essential doctrine of Christian theology, or even a clear and specific teaching of the Divine Word, since God has been pleased to keep His own counsel with reference to the possibilities of divine mercy; but as we hope and believe in the application of the benefit of Christ's redeeming work to all infants dying before they reach the age of responsibility, so we may hope and believe that there is a possibility also of the extension of this principle of grace to those of adult years among the heathen who consciously, whether under the guidance of the natural conscience or in response to the influences of the Divine Spirit, take before God an attitude of humble dependence, and seek salvation not upon the basis of merit, but upon the basis of mercy, and look to Him in penitence and prayer. God would not be God were He to turn a deaf ear to the cry of the humble penitent and trustful soul, even though that cry come out of the darkness of the heathen heart."

The spirit of the foregoing quotation accords with the true view. But there seems no reason for such cautious treatment.

It must be the dark shadow of the extreme but now fading views of Augustine and Calvin that prevents making this theory an essential doctrine of theology, and a clear teaching of the Scripture that everyone who crieth unto the Omnipotent in humility, in true penitence, whether the name of God be understood, or any special teaching from Him be recognized, is both heard and rewarded.

The Divine Being can never be justly charged with commanding the impossible, or judging men by a law that they never heard, or condemning men for stumbling in darkness in which they were born and which they were made to believe was light.

"I Also Will Show Mine Opinion"

First. Those who have never heard of the existence of one God, omnipotent, omnipresent, and

omniscient, beneficent and just, or of Christ and
His teachings, and from their birth have been
subjected to the imposition upon their minds and
hearts of elaborate religions which include many
gods and demeaning ceremonies, perverting the
understanding and deadening the conscience, cannot be held responsible for their helpless ignorance.

Second. All religions, except perhaps the very
lowest, contain some principles of morality, some
recognition of obligation to fellow men, and some
conception of moral elevation, with at least a belief that the gods will punish those who disobey,
and reward those who serve them. By their con-
sciences they are inwardly condemned or ap-
proved.

Third. The Spirit of God must move on the
hearts of all who do not willfully turn from Him;
not revealing all truth, but prompting to good
works. In this sense Christ "lighteth every man
that cometh into the world." The consequences
of denying this are set forth unanswerably by
Richard Watson:

If all knowledge of right and wrong, and all gracious
influences of the Holy Spirit, and all objects of faith
have passed away from the heathen through the fault
of their ancestors "not liking to retain God in their
knowledge," and without the present race having been
parties to this willful abandonment of truth, then they
would appear no longer to be accountable creatures,

being neither under law nor under grace; but as we find it a doctrine of Scripture that all men are responsible to God, and that the whole world will be judged at the last day, we are bound to admit the accountability of all, and with that the remains of law and the existence of a merciful government toward the heathen on the part of God.

From these principles the inevitable deduction is that those who live according to their light, longing for purity, repenting of what they believe to be sin, and treating their fellow men as the Golden Rule requires, will be admitted to the number of the saved.

Fourth. These principles underlie the New Testament. In Saint John (3. 17, 18) it is written: "God sent not his Son into the world *to condemn the world;* but *that the world through him might be saved.* He that believeth on him is not condemned; but he that believeth not is condemned already, because he hath not believed in the name of the only begotten Son of God."

This condemnation is obviously predicted of those that have learned of the only begotten Son of God, have understood His claims, but have refused His offer of salvation, not of those who never heard of Him.

In the First Epistle to the Romans Saint Paul declared that he was "a debtor both to the Greeks, and to the Barbarians"; and in Romans 2. 13-15, that "not the hearers of the law are just before

God, but the doers of the law shall be justified. For when the Gentiles, which have not the law, do by nature the things contained in the law, these, having not the law, are a law unto them selves: which show the work of the law written in their hearts, their conscience also bearing witness, and their thoughts the meanwhile accusing or else excusing one another."

In harmony with this view is Saint Peter's acceptance of Cornelius, who was not a Jew. Invited by man and commanded by God to meet the centurion, Saint Peter demurred, but his doubts were dispelled by a miraculous vision, and he said, "Of a truth I perceive that God is no respecter of persons: but in every nation he that feareth him, and worketh righteousness, is accepted with him." Attempts have been made to narrow the scope of this passage to those only who had already heard of the true God and were worshiping Him. Unquestionably, Cornelius was of that class. The principle, however, that God is "no respecter of persons" must apply to the man who is not blamable for ignorance, but lives as uprightly as his circumstances permit, maintaining the same allegiance to the powers whom he worships as conscientiously as do pious Christians to the Father, the Son, and the Holy Ghost.

Another striking instance is that of Lydia, the seller of purple in Thyatira, who worshiped God, and whose heart the Lord opened, so that she attended unto the things which were spoken of Paul. She was a proselyte made by the Jews; but if we suppose her to have been as faithful to the religion in which she was born as she was afterward to the God of Abraham, Isaac, and Jacob, and now to the religion of Christ, would she not have been accepted? To answer this question in the negative would be to impeach both the justice and the mercy of God.

Paul's address at Athens contains one passage which justifies and requires preaching to all peoples, and recognizes that migrations of the nations are not of chance, but a part of the all-inclusive plan of God. This is the clause: "And hath made of one blood all nations of men for to dwell on all the face of the earth, and hath determined the times before appointed, and the bounds of their habitation; that they should seek the Lord, if haply they might feel after him, and find him, though he be not far from every one of us." In that address he had already said: "Forasmuch then as we are the offspring of God, we ought not to think that the Godhead is like unto gold, or silver, or stone, graven by art and man's device. And the times of this ignorance God winked at; but now commandeth all men everywhere to repent."

The words "the times of this ignorance God winked at" plainly imply that those to whom the Gospel has never been made known are recognized as unable to repent, in the sense of the passage quoted.

The sense in which Christ is the Light of the whole world must be that the influence of the Holy Spirit is given to every man whether or no he has the letter of truth in his possession; and those that seek truth, and find only a mixture of it with error, are accepted by Him, if they are true to the impulses from the Spirit of God.

Wesley thus grappled the subject:

Even the heathen did not all remain in total darkness concerning the invisible and eternal world. Some few rays of light have in all ages and nations gleamed through the shade. Some light they derived from various fountains touching the invisible world. The heavens declare the glory of God, though not to their outward sight: the firmament showed to the eyes of their understanding the existence of their Maker. From the creation they infer the being of a creator powerful and wise, just and merciful. But all these lights put together avail no farther than to produce a faint twilight. It gave them, even the most intelligent of them, no demonstration, no demonstrative conviction of the invisible or eternal world.

Again, he declared that "the doctrine of Divine Providence was believed by many of the eminent heathens, not only philosophers, but orators and poets. . . . But although the ancient, as well as modern, heathens had some conception of Divine Providence, yet the conceptions which most of them entertained concerning it were dark, confused, and imperfect."

In another discourse on the passage, "Without God in the world," he says: "Let it be observed," referring to the Christian dispensation, "I have no authority from the Word of God 'to judge those that are without,' nor do I conceive that any man living has a right to sentence all the heathen and Mohammedan world to damnation. It is far better to leave them to Him that made them, and who is 'the Father of the Spirits of all flesh'; who is the God of the heathens as well as the Christians, and who hateth nothing that He has made."

Assuming, then, that such heathen will be saved as do earnestly live up to their privilege, and therefore would accept Christ should He be presented to them in a way that would illumine their partial light as the sun's rising overpowers the light of a candle, and only those rejected who are responsible, possessing normal intellectual and moral powers, yet willfully violate their own sense of right and commit gross crimes against human law, natural promptings of conscience, and every spiritual influence exerted by the God and Father of all men—the question may arise, *Why, then, need we be so concerned to save them? Why should such responsibility be placed upon us?*

There are two answers to these questions, either of which is sufficient. The first has already been detailed in the account of the benefits which the Christian has to bestow upon those vast multitudes included in the general word "heathen," and upon those who, without the excuse of ignorance, have failed to comprehend and accept the Christian standard. For such the least that philanthropy could do would be to inspire Christian nations to endeavor to persuade them to renounce their superstitions, their debasing ceremonies, and their derogatory views of those who have the highest degree of Christian civilization, and to accept the Saviour of the world.

The second answer is that the number of the saved will be greater if Christianity be preached to the non-Christian world than if not. This we find in Christian lands; the greater the light, the more intelligent and continuous the efforts of Christians to lead many to Christ, the more are converted. If a perplexed mind should ask why God did not give equal light to the human race, the answer is, "The parable of the talents must explain." If all are judged only according to their light, and the use they have made of it, who can charge the Almighty with cruelty?

Christianity demands that we carry the Gospel to those who are destitute of it, and light to them that sit in darkness, and the more light, the greater will be the number of the finally saved.

"For whosoever shall call upon the name of the Lord shall be saved. How then shall they call on him in whom they have not believed? and how shall they believe in him of whom they have not heard? and how shall they hear without a preacher? and how shall they preach except they be sent? as it is written, How beautiful are the feet of them that preach the gospel of peace, and bring glad tidings of good things!"

Throughout the inspired record, like a solemn toll, sounds the insistent refrain, "GO PREACH."

THE SECOND LECTURE

METHODS, MEANS, AND MEN OF CHRISTIAN MISSIONS

THE SECOND LECTURE

METHODS, MEANS, AND MEN OF CHRISTIAN MISSIONS

RELATIVE to Foreign Missions the Christian world may best be considered in three grand divisions: the Latin, or Roman Catholic Church, the Greek Church, and the Protestant Church.

A SURVEY

In the time of Peter the Great the orthodox Greek Church was divided into two bodies, one retaining the original name, the other popularly called the Russo-Greek Church, which is identified in the vast Russian empire. The third division is the orthodox Protestant Churches. The heterodox Protestant Communions have few missions. The words "orthodox" and "heterodox" are used here for want of better terms to indicate the difference. Those designated "heterodox," among other differences, deny the deity of Christ, the orthodox relation of His death and sufferings to the salvation of mankind, His resurrection, and the probationary character of life.

The Roman Catholic Church has missions in every part of the world. Comparatively little mission work has been done for the last four

hundred years by the Oriental Churches included
in the orthodox Greek Church.   The Russian
empire, about two hundred years ago, added the
whole northern part of Asia; and the Russian National Church has done a missionary work which,
though imperfect, is recognized by discriminating
writers "as one of the most important triumphs
of the cross in the whole period of modern Missions."   The outlying spurs of the movement are
seen in the Aleutian Islands and Alaska.   Nearly
all the strictly foreign mission work of the Russo-
Greek Church is in Japan, where it has prospered.

The missionary enterprises of Protestantism
for many decades were included in the colonial
undertakings of the nations which revolted from
Roman Catholicism.   Such were the operations
of the French reformers in Brazil, Gustavus Vasa
in Lapland, and of the Dutch East India Company (which in one of the articles of its charter
avowed the purpose of converting the heathen),
and of the early missionary efforts of England.
Sir Walter Raleigh dispatched a man of piety to
Virginia, and money was contributed "in special
regard and zeal of planting a Christian religion
in those dark countries."

In the charter of Charles I to the Massachusetts Company the king's hope was expressed that
"the colony would win the natives of the country

to the knowledge and obedience of the true God and Saviour of mankind." A most striking fact is the action of the Long Parliament, which passed an ordinance July 27, 1649, legalizing "a corporation for promoting and propagating the Gospel of Jesus Christ in New England."

The Society for Promoting Christian Knowledge was established two hundred and ten years ago, its chief work being the distribution of Bibles and other books of Christian doctrine, life, and history.

Three years later was formed "The Society for the Propagation of the Gospel in Foreign Parts." The charter granted by William III specified that it is "for the purpose of receiving, managing, and dispensing of funds contributed for the religious instruction of the queen's subjects beyond the seas, for the maintenance of clergymen in the plantations, colonies, and factories of Great Britain, and for the propagation of the Gospel in those parts."

General Methods of Organization

Some Protestant Churches incorporated with the State carry on missionary work effectively: for example, the Church of England, the Established Church of Scotland, the Lutheran Churches in Germany, and the Church of Holland. And where there are National Churches, Dissenting, and Non-Conformists, they enjoy comparative independent liberty of action. In free countries there are denominations, organized on the principle that the smaller branches are governed by central delegated bodies. Examples of this are the different Communions under the Presbyterian form of government, the different Methodist denominations of the United States, and the United Kingdom of Great Britain and Ireland. Such are the constantly growing Lutheran organizations in this country, the most widely known being the General Council and the General Synod.

Other Churches invest the power in the local congregation, which is indicated by the name "Congregational"; and the same rule prevails in the Baptist collection of Churches, and in the large body known as the Disciples of Christ.

It will be conceded that the principles essential to the success of any missionary endeavor are substantial unity of doctrine and spirit, for how can two "walk together" or work together "except they be agreed"?

An illustration of the marvelous efficiency of a central authority is found in the history of Roman Catholic missions. For a hundred and twenty-five years, beginning in 1500, they were practically unorganized and carried on work independently. Unsurpassed heroism and sacrifice of life mark that long history, without commensurate results. Only two years after the Pilgrims landed in New England the far-famed Congregation of the Propaganda was established in Rome, and it has entire control of nearly all the missionary undertakings of the Roman Catholic Church. Its affairs are regulated by the College of the Cardinals, in the center of which have sat the successive Popes, preserving a unity in operation and a vigor in action which, whatever may be thought of its claims and methods, deserves the admiration of the civilized world.

Efforts to maintain a similar central authority have been made by all religious Communions, but of necessity have been modified by the radical distinctions of government, civil and ecclesiastic.

The Russo-Greek Church is more closely incorporated with the empire than is any other Church with a civil government. The Czar is its head; the Holy Synod is an arm alike of the religious and secular government, and controls the missionary enterprises of the Church, the money for their support being appropriated from the treasury of the empire.

The normal order is that in every closely organized denomination, and in every State Church, missionary undertakings should be managed by the Church as the center of authority and direction.

This was the plan for many years in all State

Churches, so that it is difficult, to distinguish historically their purely missionary operations. On this account more credit is probably due them for missionary work, in the early periods of the Reformation, than is generally accorded.

Yet if there be well-defined radical variance of belief or ceremony in the bosom of a State Church, it may be far better for Missionary Societies to operate through corporations. It is obvious that there are such differences of view in the Church of England as to make it impossible for those holding them (with the exception of a few minds of peculiarly liberal cast or unusual adaptive facility) to work together satisfactorily.

Thoroughly organized denominations unconnected with the State are managed by their own missionary organizations, subject to the highest authority in the Church. This they must do to secure universal financial sympathy. But such support, however, will be dissipated or diverted to independent enterprises, and sufficient latent ability and means will never be elicited without universal pastoral instruction and persuasion. This cannot be maintained unless the missionary spirit pervades the Church and controls to a high degree its legislation on the subject.

If these principles be true, they must find abundant illustration in all organized denominations.

CONFIRMATION OF THE FOREGOING

Thus we find the *Church Missionary Society*, founded April 12, 1799, for sending the Gospel of Christ to the heathen and to the Mohammedan world, whether within or without the dominions of Great Britain. It is strictly a Church of England Society, conducted by a patron, vice-patron, president, vice-president, and a committee. These must be members of the Established Church of England or of the Church of Ireland. The patron must be a member of the royal family, the vice-patron His Grace the Primate of all England. The president may be a temporal peer or a commoner, and the vice-presidents shall consist of such archbishops and bishops of the Churches of England and Ireland who belong to the Society and will accept that office. The committee consists of twenty-five lay members of the Society, who must be members of the Church of England or the Church of Ireland, and of all churchmen or clergymen who have been members of the Society for at least one year. There are other officers ex officio members of the committee.

Under the authority of the law of the land, the bishops of the Church of England ordain and send forth the Society's missionaries; and in the event of their being appointed by the committee, they are to labor on stations within the jurisdiction of a bishop of the Church of England. The Society applies to the bishops for licenses, in which are specified the districts to which the missionaries have been assigned.

To prevent disturbances between the committee and local bishops, all questions that may arise of ecclesiastical order and discipline are referred to any tribunal having cognizance of the same; but if not, they are to be referred to the Archbishops of Canterbury and York, who have final authority.

The Church Missionary Society, though belonging to the Church of England, has traditions as well as laws. "The Church Missionary Society is downright evangelical in its traditions, and that cannot honestly be said of the whole Church of England. Therefore," says the editorial secretary of the Church Missionary Society of London, "it is practically a Society of an exceptional character, representing a section of the Church. If the bishops or any other great authorities in Church or State, any authority whatever, were to tell the Church Missionary Society's committee, or the Church Missionary Society as a body, to do anything contrary to evangelical principles, its constituency would rise as one man and refuse."

This seems an admirable arrangement, and no doubt accounts very largely for the enthusiasm, immense contributions, and general success of the Church Missionary Society.

Denominations which deposit final authority in the local church must coöperate through societies created for the purpose by means of boards of managers more or less limited in jurisdiction. Of these, the most renowned in the Western Hemisphere is the *American Board of Commissioners for Foreign Missions,* which was organized in 1810 by the General Association of Congregational Ministers of Massachusetts. It was professedly undenominational, and in its early days was coöperated with by several other denominations, especially the Presbyterian, but the different bodies having gradually formed for themselves missionary societies, it is now left almost wholly under the control of the Congregational Churches.

The American Board has conspicuously demonstrated the possibility of achieving great success by means of what is, to all intents and purposes, a strictly voluntary organization.

There is a remarkable similarity between the history of this body and that of the *London Missionary Society*, which was originally undenominational, having been founded by evangelical members of the Church of England, Presbyterian bodies, and Congregationalists. The London Missionary Society is fifteen years older than the American Board of Commissioners for Foreign Missions, and has passed into the hands of Congregationalists exclusively for the same reason, namely, the formation of missionary societies in most of the Churches whose members originally coöperated with it. These two bodies are among the most successful missionary organizations in the world.

Four years after the American Board was founded the *American Baptist Missionary Society* was formed. It grew out of the change of sentiment concerning the subjects and mode of baptism experienced by Adoniram Judson and Luther Rice, who had been sent out by the American Board.

For thirty years all the missionary work of American Baptists was done through the *Baptist General Convention,* afterward known as the *Triennial.* This gave rise to the establishment of the *American Baptist Missionary Union,* organized in 1846. It is composed of delegates, but the real business is done by a Board of Managers, of whom one third are elected at each annual meeting, and by an Executive Committee chosen by this Board.

As already stated, prior to 1837 the members of the Presbyterian Church in the United States

coöperated largely with the American Board of
Commissioners for Foreign Missions. Since then
it has had its own society, which is incorporated
in the State of New York. The Act declares that
the management and disposition of the affairs and
property of the said Board of Foreign Missions
of the *Presbyterian Church in the United States
of America* shall be vested in twenty-one trustees,
who shall be appointed from time to time by
the *General Assembly of the Presbyterian Church
in the United States of America,* for such terms
as the Assembly may determine.

The Board of Foreign Missions reports annually, and surrenders its entire records to the
General Assembly for investigation. The General
Assembly refers the same to a standing committee, which body examines the records, and, it
necessary, makes a detailed scrutiny of all transactions. This society is as thoroughly incorporated with the Church as is possible, and the results of its operation, in unity, receipts, and
efficiency, are in proportion to the closeness of
its incorporation.

In a similar manner the business of the *Foreign
Missions of the Reformed Church* in the United
States is conducted. The powers of the Board of
Commissioners elected by the General Synod are
absolute—provided they are not repugnant to the
Constitution of the United States, the Constitu-

tion of Pennsylvania, or the Constitution of the General Synod of the Reformed Church in the United States.

The Missionary Society of the Methodist Episcopal Church is similarly mortised into the body and cemented into the life of the Church. Its Board of Managers is appointed by the General Conference, which invests the Board with power to fill vacancies. The General Conference also elects the corresponding secretary, the assistant corresponding secretary, the treasurer, and the assistant treasurer, and it reserves to itself the power of at any time amending the Constitution of the Society; and the Act of Incorporation given by the State of New York provides that the Board of Managers shall be subordinate to any directions made or to be made by the said General Conference. That body also elects a *General Missionary Committee* which alone has power to establish new missions, to close missions, and to determine the amount of money which shall be appropriated to each mission. The Board of Managers by the charter holds all missionary property of the Church throughout the world, and all specific property of the Church.

This system had worked so admirably that when the Methodist Episcopal Church, South, was formed in 1845 it adopted substantially the same method.

The *Wesleyan Missionary Society of England,*
after many individual and local efforts, was organized in 1818. Conditions of membership were
adopted by the Conference, which appoints a committee intrusted with the general management of
the missions and the raising and disbursing of
money, subject to the general rules and usages of
the connection. The treasurers and the general
secretaries are also elected by the Conference, the
governing body of the denomination. The Wesleyan Methodist Missionary Society has a more
detailed and comprehensive system of rules for
the management of Missions throughout the
Church than can be found elsewhere in Protestantism.

The Moravian Church, incorporated in the
commonwealth of Pennsylvania in 1788, is practically a society for propagating the Gospel. Its
highest body, the General Synod, is composed of
representatives of all provinces and of missions.
It elects the Unity's Elders' Conference, which is
charged with the administration of the missions
and other joint affairs. The Directing Board is
responsible to the General Synod of the Unity of
the Brethren for the whole range of its actions
and management.

The Moravians have the credit of being really
the pioneer non-Roman Catholic mission Church.
By 1750 they had established more missions than

all other Protestants combined in the preceding two hundred years.

From the nature of the case, *undenominational* and *private organizations* are independent of the government of any one denomination. The *China Inland Mission* is the most conspicuous example of this method of missionary labor. It was founded by J. Hudson Taylor in 1865, with the financial help and coöperation of W. T. Burger. Mr. Taylor was, until his death, general director, and was assisted by those who, at his invitation, were associated with him in the conduct of the work. "It is supported by the free-will offerings of the Lord's people." The directors cannot and do not guarantee any fixed amount of support for the missions and missionaries. During Hudson Taylor's life it was governed by a personal head, as really as was Methodism in its early days by Wesley, and as the Salvation Army is by William Booth.

In the different organizations of Lutherans in the United States various methods obtain in the management of Missionary Societies, some not radically different from those already described; others come properly under a different classification.

An examination of the Constitutions of German and Scandinavian Protestant missions re-

veals no methods of organizing missions which
do not exist elsewhere.

A comparison of the charters, constitutions,
by-laws, and reports of the principal societies in
Great Britain, Ireland, and Canada, the conti-
nent of Europe, and the United States abundantly
justifies the following generalizations:

CONDITIONS OF SUCCESS

The success of boards of foreign missions subordinate to religious Communions depends upon
the selection and revision of executive boards.
Rich men who give nothing but money, and rich
men who give nothing but counsel, and poor men
who give nothing but attendance on board meetings, can do little except to aid in making a
quorum. Men of substance who give sympathy,
counsel, intelligent scrutiny, and money; poor
men who bring wisdom in counsel, and vigilance,
and give according to the gifts of God to them,
and men who are neither rich nor poor, but competent and interested, should compose a majority
of every such board. Assemblies, conferences,
councils, conventions, or synods should not be
content with the perfunctory reference of the reports of missionary boards to a committee who
will approve indiscriminately and recommend a
rising vote of thanks.

In the denominations, which from the nature of

their government must work through societies
formed for the purpose, more importance should
be attached to the competency of the commissioners or managers than to popular oratory—although that gift is to be greatly valued if connected with the stable qualities necessary for
security.

The reflex influence of the board upon the denomination is powerful according to the work and
personality of the managers and their secretaries.
If it may energize, it may also paralyze. Boards
as servants and guides give the best results;
boards as tyrants are shackles.

Some societies, depending on one or two individuals, have done and still are doing good,
though a large majority have failed, and *others
have wasted many thousands of the Lord's money
while boasting of the superiority of their methods
over those of other churches.*

In general, the only communicants of Christian Churches who can consistently support *undenominational* societies are those who conscientiously and regularly support the missionary work
of their own religious Communion.

Financial Problems and Property Titles

Comparatively few in the churches comprehend
the responsibilities of boards of management.
Only a minority of business establishments can

compare in details, difficulties, and contingencies with those of Missionary Boards. They fix the salaries and determine the work of all employees; hold the deeds of all property; are liable to be sued, and are frequently compelled to sue. They receive bequests, frequently involving vexatious conditions; hold deeds of all property throughout the world; and are compelled to sit in judgment upon transactions conducted in foreign languages and under legal restrictions unknown to their thought and practice. They accept or refuse the offer of annuities; and, therefore, must consider whether the principal will afford the interest promised, or, if not, whether the health and age of the person to whom the interest is paid is likely to consume or greatly diminish the principal. On them also is the responsibility of seeing that those which are accepted are sacredly guarded, and the annuitants promptly paid.

To protect their important properties in foreign lands the title must rest in boards of trustees in the home country. Only thus can foreign nations be compelled to indemnify missions for the destruction suffered by the failure of their government to protect them against riot and rapine, or its complicity in the same. The destruction caused by the Boxer attacks upon missions is an object lesson in connection with this part of the responsibilities of the Board.

These bodies must make the appropriations for the year. They are, in truth, "faith" institutions; their members have faith in the Church, the stability of their country's finances, and the providence of God. They must superintend the raising of funds early in the fiscal year, or immediately before it begins.

There are those who proclaim loudly that they "depend wholly upon God and never ask anyone to give." But that very proclamation is a subtle form of begging, resembling the inconsistency of a beggar who plants himself upon the front steps of a mansion, saying to all that pass by, "I will never ask for food, but unless some one gives it to me I shall die of starvation."

In view of the fact that they have not in hand the money which will make good the appropriations, Missionary Boards must have credit at the banks and means of securing those banks. Credit depends, in considerable part, upon the amount and kind of property that the Society owns—its reputation for good management and a trustworthy constituency.

It is necessary for a large Missionary Society to own property, to keep it in repair, and to invest the moneys that are constantly coming in. But the funds annually raised for Missions are not, as are the revenues of the country, brought in under the threat of the sale of their property if they do not pay their taxes, or as fraternal societies secure their funds. From the widow's mite to the resources of wealthy members of the Church all that the Missionary Society receives is a free gift, which may be larger or smaller, according to the ability of the donor or his caprice. When the death of the head of a family occurs, and a large estate is divided among the widow and children, even though all continue to support in some degree the missionary cause, the sum total is generally less than that given by the head of the family in his lifetime. Panics also unfavorably affect the gifts of employers, and more so those of employees, and strikes and lockouts have a marvelously shrinking effect upon missionary collections.

Vital Elements

But more difficult is the selection of missionaries, the determining their salaries, the length of their vacations, their superannuation, their furloughs, provision for their families, the settling of feuds in missions, and the removing of missionaries. This consumes a vast amount of time, and requires investigation by correspondence, and not unfrequently by an expensive visit to the field by a secretary or a special commissioner. It is apparent that the raising of funds for Missionary Societies requires a rare combination of abilities and endless perseverance.

Pastors must be the most prominent agents; and if the missionary cause were the only one which they were obliged to present to their congregations, the task would be comparatively easy. But when, upon an average, they are obliged to exhort the people to make contributions to as many causes as there are months in the year, to say nothing of special emergencies, their vocabulary and their voices become monotonous. The missionary secretaries and the boards must supplement through various agencies ordinary sources of information and stimulus. In England it is not uncommon for a clergyman to ask one of his brethren to deliver the annual missionary sermon in his pulpit, compensating him by a similar service, each being at home when the other presents the cause. Loyalty to the church, the effect on the pastor's standing, the dissemination of vivid and authentic incidents pertaining to the situation must be emphasized.

And since every philanthropic and religious enterprise of importance has an organ, it is necessary for the Missionary Societies to employ the press. A weak organ, like a somnolent speech, is worse than silence or blank paper.

It is very desirable that at least one secretary be an eloquent presenter of the cause. It has been

said that no *merely* eloquent man ever produced
a permanent effect or brought anything of importance to pass. But, assuming that they have
common sense, eloquent men, associated with men
of talent ready for persevering work, may accomplish much. The ideal missionary secretary
should combine an ingratiating personality, the
faculty of interesting statement, and at least fair
ability and judgment for the work of the office.

Fortunately, the standing and character of secretaries usually guarantees peace and brotherly
kindness between them and the committees and
boards. But as Saul and Barnabas fell into a dis-
sension which separated them for a time, so there
may be difficulty which adds to the responsibilities
and work of the Board.

The Selection of Missionaries

Special attention has been attracted of late
years to the methods of selecting missionaries to
foreign peoples. In former times difficulties and
danger prevented the timid from soliciting a place
upon a missionary staff. Voyages were long,
salaries small, perils great; so that, speaking generally, only those called of God, or of a very in-
trepid and adventurous nature, desired the position.

At present a sufficient number can be obtained
to man the missions. But persons are of all types.

Some have applied for the sake of an excursion;
under the appeals of a foreign missionary some
have felt called of God; or the plaintive voice of
a woman physician describing the dreadful
scenes with which her profession brings her in contact may make a similar impression; and some,
with emotion enough, are without energy, and
destitute of tact.

In achieving the college valedictory in the colleges some have lost what may be called external
energy. Others are already physically ill, yet un-
aware of it until subjected to the regular medical examination. Others are encumbered by
small children, whose sickness at any time may
break up the family. Some have every qualification except the gift for acquiring languages;
and others possess no other qualification than
that.

A standard has been advocated in various quar-
ters which is too high for the average require-
ments, while some standards are much too low.
In every large mission there should be several men
competent to be presidents of seminaries or colleges. The average missionaries in any country
should be such as could not be sneered at as igno-
ramuses, satirized as boors, despised as neglect-
ers of duty, or shunned as intermeddlers with the
harmless peculiarities of the natives or with missions of other denominations. It is essential that

each missionary have at least the germs of financial success, and necessary to guard against acceptance of ministers who have not succeeded in whatever pastoral efforts they may have made.

As a principle, it is wise not to take the graduate of a theological seminary or a college who has had no experience in a pastorate, unless, indeed, he be intended solely or chiefly for a professorship in an institution.

The superanuation of missionaries is frequently a heartrending process; to remove them even more so. But these, as in all other spheres, are difficulties which, if not met, will be the source of greater trouble.

ELEMENTS OF SUCCESS IN DEALING WITH NON-CHRISTIAN PEOPLES

Originally the Gospel spread mainly by a sort of natural radiation from the centers in which it had first been preached. We must not forget that the apostles went everywhere. When Paul heard the Macedonian cry he did not respond that there were many still in the place where he then was who had not been brought to Christ; but whatever the apostles taught believers they transmitted to their heathen neighbors. It is authentic history that Celsus spoke scornfully of shoemakers and fullers who talked about their doctrines in their workshops. During the reign of Decius seven missionary bishops left Rome to labor in the yet unevangelized parts of Gaul. When Constantine and Licinius met at Milan early in 313 a curious edict was issued in their joint names proclaiming religious toleration to all religions, "that so the Deity, or Heavenly Being, whatever it is, may be propitious both to ourselves and all our subjects."

Ireland in 493 had become Christian. In Britain were two heathen kingdoms of Kent and Sussex, and the rest of the island was partly Christian and partly Druid.

The sixth century might be called an age of Missions; all followed the example of Paul and Silas; they were courteous, every opportunity was utilized, and as soon as any large section was Christianized native missionaries seized every advantage in surrounding regions. "It may safely be affirmed that there are few of the difficulties against which missionaries have to contend which do not find a parallel in the story of their earlier prototypes."

Celibacy or Matrimony for Missionaries

It cannot be doubted that Roman Catholic enterprises derive great benefit from the enforced celibacy of the priests and deacons; whereas the illness of a wife or of a child may necessitate long absences from the mission, filling the heart of the missionary, who remains, with distracting anxiety, there are also many instances when common humanity requires the transport of the whole family to the homeland. In most mission fields the climate has to be reckoned a steady or capricious enemy of the health of foreigners, and, in the aggregate, many missionaries must be located far from satisfactory medical facilities.

The wife of the missionary may never have contemplated a removal from the country in which her parents reside. When her husband is called to the mission field, and entreats her, love for him and belief in his call to the work constrains her to go; but her interests are divided. Instances have occurred of the refusal of a wife to accompany her husband, or to remain after reaching the field.

Should all be sympathy and peace, the question of the higher education for the children arises. And the later question of the "social realm," in which the sons and daughters may find congenial helpmates, without being fully recognized as the controlling impulse, doubles the attractive force toward the land whence they came.

The celibate priest can be removed, without damage to his working capacity, from one point to a very remote one within the bounds of the mission to which he was first sent, or to another, or to found a new mission in another part of the world, with the least possible expense.

It is believed by Protestants generally—with which I agree—that all these disadvantages are countervailed by the presentation of the Christian family to polygamist peoples, and to those in which women are doomed to assumed inferiority, made *actual* by the refusal to them of education, and the privilege of the status of woman, as described in the Christian Scriptures.

Nevertheless, the selection of missionaries requires surveillance from the beginning: without doubt there is sometimes laxity and carelessness in examination.

Young men, early married, with small children, are discounted by the facts when they apply for the denominational missionary commission. In every case the prospective missionary and his wife should be subject to medical examination, at least as thorough as that demanded for life insurance. Among the saddest experiences of boards of management is the duty, sometimes heart-breaking in its effect upon the subject, of declaring the physical risk too great.

The spiritual risk, also, has to be taken into account. If the wife have no special sympathy with the work to which the husband goes, only a great emergency would justify his employment.

In the judgment of many it is desirable to find a proportion of missionaries who will forego thoughts of matrimony for the cause. It must be admitted, however, that in several such cases, surrounded by an aureole of splendid spiritual heroism, men have met on the field or in the families of residents attractions so great as to cause them to believe that their efficiency would be greatly increased by wedlock. In some instances missionaries have found themselves so lonely as to give the secretaries at home commissions to select for them Christian women desiring the mission field, who, if congenial, would marry. Exchanges of photographs supplied the only knowledge each received of the other's physiognomy, and correspondence the only medium of communication, until the bride to be arrived on the mission field. Sometimes this union has been very happy, and the mission and the missionary greatly reënforced. Failures, however, placed a sense of responsibility upon the missionary secretaries which weighed so heavily upon them that this form of mediation has been suffered to sink into "innocuous desuetude."

Individual evangelistic methods are not reducible to a system of universal application.

How different the process of Christianizing the Fiji Islands, the American Indians, the Eskimos, from that necessary in India, China or Japan! In all exist the original elements of intellectual intercourse, moral persuasion and religion, human fears and loves. The wildest tribes possess will, memory, imagination, reason, conscience, the emotions of love and hate.

A great evolution has taken place in missionary methods in every country where missions have long been established. It was at first a hand-to-hand moral and intellectual conflict. Signs were used before words could be understood. Later, the vernacular began to be mastered: missionaries stumbled, but, in their stumbling, learned. As soon as churches were organized, and Christian families arose, schools became necessary; teachers were to be qualified; and next to the school came the seminary. But as native preachers and teachers were needed, colleges to furnish professors for the seminaries were demanded by the same forces which have originated them in Christian nations.

SHOULD CONVERTS BE SENT TO CHRISTIAN LANDS FOR EDUCATION FOR THE MINISTRY?

A question of large importance has arisen. Should brilliant minds among missionary converts be sent to America, England, or Germany for education, or should they be trained in institutions founded by the missions and conducted in their native tongues? On this subject no law as

fixed as that of the Medes and Persians can
be made.   Certain natives of peculiar tempera-
ment, grasp of intellect, and notable for prudence
and caution, may derive great benefit by higher
education in the land and under the auspices of
the Church founding the mission.   But it would
be a miracle if the majority could be trusted in
their youth, at least, to return better qualified for
the evangelization of their kindred and countrymen.   What must be its effect upon a convert who
explores the world and comes in close contact with
all forms of rationalistic unbelief ? In schools, colleges, and theological seminaries supported by the
very religious Communion which sent out the
men who, under God, were the means of the conversion of these students, some promising young
men have been practically ruined for Christian
native ministers and professors.   They have been
injured by pride of knowledge and became ar-
rogant when among their kindred.

It would be easy to add to these considerations
some others worthy of note, but it is hardly necessary.   Whatever may be the wisdom of a century
later in the evolution of Missions, it may be
affirmed with adequate foundation that only in
rare cases should unsophisticated converts from
other religions, who are useful in the schools established by the missions, be sent to the country which
maintains the mission.

Special Modern Helps

Industrial schools are sometimes very valuable; but they are not so if they do not afford an opportunity for religious instruction. In Africa they have been found "eminently helpful in giving direction to life. . . . They seem to rescue young lives from inanity and idleness, and give them a start in a career of self-respecting usefulness, with the Gospel planted in their hearts" (Dennis, on Foreign Missions After a Century, p. 234).

Medical missions are invaluable in almost every unchristianized region, and in such undeveloped countries as Mexico and various parts of South America. In China, Japan, India, South America, and Mexico, as well as in the countries of southeastern Europe, they have been of the highest efficiency. Where nothing else could open doors for evangelization, the medical mission was the sesame to Christianity. From the lips of Li Hung Chang I received a testimonial as to the work and value of the medical missions established by the Methodist Episcopal Church in China, so comprehensive and unequivocal as to carry conviction to any mind, especially, when in his own family he had received an administration of relief, which led him to make a large con-

tribution to one of the Methodist hospitals. Other
denominations testify to similar results. Dr.
Dennis thus covers the whole case:

"The place of medical work, if done with Christian sympathy and tact, and followed up with
Christian instruction, is vindicated both by the
example of Christ, and by all experience. In the
hands of lady physicians it is at present practically the only method of reaching the women in
many heathen communities" (Foreign Missions
After a Century, pp. 233, 234). I have studied
these hospitals in operation in various parts of the
Turkish empire, and seen the Christian American side by side with the Mohammedan Egyp-
tian or Arabian. The present method in those
hospitals is not to force Christianity upon the
patients, but so to impregnate the social atmos-
phere with its spirit as to make it understood that
that spirit is the cause and support of the healing
benefactions.

An interesting question has arisen on account
of the marvelous success of these hospitals in comparison with that of native physicians unin-
structed in Western surgery and medicine, mental
and physical. Shall the well-to-do native be expected to pay surgeons and physicians for his
treatment? This has been discussed widely in
England, and the conclusion seems to be that it
is better for patients to do so than to have the

impression that the services rendered are of no
great value, and under the idea that they are objects of charity. It would appear, however, that
unless the patient be willing to pay, it would be
a hazardous experiment to compel him, as he
might easily use the fact to the detriment of confidence in the motives of the missionaries.

WORK OF WOMEN'S SOCIETIES

The work of women organized under the various women's foreign missionary societies is the
admiration of all who have seen it. Attention has
naturally been given in large measure to women
and children. Its institutions are numerous and
success great. Its methods are practically the
same, so far as the work is in common with that
of the general missionary societies. Many of the
missionary wives are engaged in its work. Its
plans of raising money are eminently successful;
its schools are admirably managed and bounti-
fully supported. Its work is usually in places
where there are already missions. Thus they are
protected, and find in the few instances when they
come in collision with native authorities the entire denominational influence ready to support
them against imposition.

To the Rev. David Abeel, D.D., an American
missionary to China, must be conceded the honor
of suggesting to Christian women the importance

of a *distinctive* mission for heathen women. His
zeal and eloquence resulted, in 1834, in the organization, in England, of the Society for Female
Education in the East, "and, seconded by the appeals of Mrs. Francis B. Mason, of Burma, in the
establishment January 15, 1861, of the Woman's
Union Missionary Society for Heathen Lands."
These are the pioneers of women's organized distinctive work for women. In that Missionary
Society women of six denominations composed its
membership; it stood alone for eight years; then
the Woman's Board of Missions (Congregational)
of Boston was organized. The Woman's Foreign
Missionary Society of the Methodist Episcopal
Church was organized in March, 1869. An Eng-
lishman writes:

"The reports of women's societies in the old
country seldom have anything to say of the children's part in the modern missionary crusade;
but in the United States and Canada they are a
great factor. The children are organized into
bands, of which they are themselves officers. . . .
One of the first momentous duties of a band is to
name itself, and the English language has been
explored for the purpose. There are the Carrier
Doves and Lookout Guards, Snowflakes and May-
flowers, Busy Bees, Steady Streams, Mustard
Seeds, King's Cadets, Up and Readys, Little
Lights, Pearl Seekers, Acorns, The Drum Corps,

Do What You Can Band, and so on, in endless
variety."

In manning schools, colleges, universities, and
medical missions it is vital that presidents, professors, and all in authority shall be Christians.
They need not, in every case, be of the Communion
supporting the institutions, but they should be
unmistakably Christian, in faith, spirit, and conduct; for one agnostic or frivolous talker upon
spiritual things can not only work much evil but
vitiate much good.

CHRIST'S METHOD OF APPROACH NOT OUTWORN

It is almost universally conceded that the methods of Christ and the apostles are, in essence, not
only safe models for missionaries but the most
fruitful. Our Lord spoke with an authority that
astonished all, and supported it by miracles. The
apostles also had the power of working miracles,
yet though there is a marked difference between
our Lord's manner in approaching men, and the
apostles themselves recognized His absolute command, there is in their manner the manifestation
of a consciousness of authority given to them by
our Lord.

What can be more uncompromising than the
address of Peter to his countrymen on the day of
Pentecost? Yet it is interspersed by such pas-

sages as, "Men and brethren, let me freely speak
unto you of the patriarch David"; and, again,
"For the promise is unto you, and to your children, and to all that are afar off"; and, again,
"And now, brethren, I wot that through ignorance ye did it, as did also your rulers." Stephen
was stern, fearfully so at times, as was Christ, for
such holy indignation is needed.

How beautiful is the conversation of Philip
with the eunuch, how pertinent that of Ananias
with Paul, and of Peter with Cornelius; of Paul
and Barnabas among the Greeks; and Paul's manner and words before Felix and Festus, and, above
all, Agrippa; and what dignity, approaching
majesty, of the speech to the philosophers at
Athens! The Epistles show clear penetration
and sound judgment in determining the best
method of inducting men into the knowledge and
life of Christ.

The best summary thereof in the fewest words
is in the Appendix to the remarkable volume entitled Islam and Christianity in India and the
Far East, by Dr. E. M. Wherry, for thirty years
missionary of the Presbyterian Church in India.
This work comprises the Student Lectures on Missions at Princeton Theological Seminary for
1906-07. I quote some of his maxims, omitting
his comments:

"Religious controversy on missionary ground

is attended by serious evils, such as the arousing of prejudice, the possible strengthening of conviction in error, and the creation of a party spirit." But, "properly conducted, it emphasizes the points of difference between the true and the false, serves to fix the truth in minds open to doubt, makes necessary a definite statement of principles involved, and calls popular attention to the questions under discussion."

To prevent the evils controversy should not be carried on in the open bazaar. "The men who are ever ready to debate in such a place are hardly ever men who seek to know the truth." Nor should it be allowed in the course of a chapel service. Let the chapel service be held sacred to the cause of Christian preaching.

Nor should controversy be indulged during a personal call. "A social call should be made to serve the interests of good will and friendship." The subject of religion should not be tabooed, for such a call may afford the best opportunity for religious converse; but that is different from a debate "which may degenerate into offensive speech which would break asunder the ties of friendship." "The least sign of angry feeling should be the sign to stop." If the missionary gives way to anger, he "has practically been defeated." "No point should ever be discussed until it has been definitely stated." No trivial question should be discussed. "Whenever the opposition fails to disclose a serious desire to learn or maintain what he believes to be the truth, debate should be declined." "Never should subjects be discussed in public if they are calculated to arouse angry passion; but religious discussion may be held at any time and at any place fixed upon by mutual consent." It should be on a subject previously announced and clearly defined, "and never be undertaken unless there is a reasonable hope that it can be conducted in a calm and dispassionate manner." "In dealing with Mohammedans, Buddhists, Confucianists, success depends, first of all, upon very careful preparation. The missionary, lay or clerical, should always preserve a good temper and a serious mood." "It is all-important to give one's opponent full opportunity to express his views." "In religious controversy argument should, as far as possible, be based on the Bible and the books which opponents regard as sacred or authoritative."

Dr. Wherry emphasizes some plain rules which are as applicable to all countries, languages, religions, nations, and every possible kind of discussion: "Be sure of your opponent's position. Be fair to your opponent. Hold fast to the main issue. Always avoid any appearance of joy or exultation over the defeat or perplexity of an adversary."

He gives special cautions to Christians conducting discussions by the pen: "The writer should be respectful in language and address, and should be sympathetic." The other is a fine lesson for all religious controversial writers: "Let all matters be presented in a discursory manner. The danger of the average writer is that he will destroy the influence of his writing by assuming a dogmatic style. But if we discuss all sides of the question at issue, stating as strongly as possible the positions claimed by our opponent and meeting by anticipation his argument, we not only secure a better hearing—or, rather, reading—but we forestall any charge of unfairness or one-sidedness in argument. Every advance in argument should be made in a scholarly manner, demolishing the enemy's defenses as we go, and building upon their ruins the edifice of Christian truth."

These directions were not all originally conceived by Dr. Wherry, for some of them were enforced upon us by instructors long since deceased. We have substantially quoted from him because some of his suggestions are purely original, and also for the purpose of presenting his testimony regarding the dangers, the benefits, and the methods of religious controversy in non-Christian lands.

It may seem incongruous to close this important part of the subject by a quotation from Con-

fucius, but it is pertinent. "If you do not learn
the rules of propriety, your character cannot be
established. . . . If you are grave, you will not
be treated with disrespect; if you are generous,
you will win all; if you are sincere, people will
repose trust in you; if you are earnest, you will
accomplish much; if you are kind, this will enable
you to employ the services of others."

THE THIRD LECTURE

A JUDICIAL COMPARISON OF CIRCUMSTANCES UNFAVORABLE AND FAVORABLE TO PRESENT-DAY FOREIGN MISSION WORK

THE THIRD LECTURE

THE aim of this lecture is to make a judicial comparison between circumstances favorable and unfavorable to present mission work.

ELEVEN GRIEVOUS OBSTACLES

One evil is the nonattendance, except at rare intervals, of a proportion of members of boards. These are frequently the busiest of men, and often the best qualified to give advice upon the numerous and complex financial problems. A distinguished layman of New York, director in several corporations and banking institutions, and the head of a manufacturing concern employing four thousand operatives, finding that he was neglecting the missionary interest, while much attached to it, determined upon placing meetings of the Board of Managers on his list of regular engagements; and from that time to the close of his life found no more difficulty in being present there than at institutions more closely allied to his personal and pecuniary enterprises, and he was no less faithful to the latter than before.

Another evil is the tendency of boards to involve the Society in debt, which is usually brought about in the following way: Some prominent member or officer becomes especially interested in a particular mission, and proposes a great advance in the appropriations. Then the friends of that mission and the advocates of an advance along the entire line, unite; the conservatives speak, but their efforts to put on the brakes are not as strong or persuasive as that of those whose refrain is, "Can't you trust God?" and by a majority all the indications of a financial storm are ignored.

Occasionally, another serious danger is that women's societies may draw too heavily on the common reservoir of the Church's wealth and willingness. Instances have occurred where in local churches the Woman's Foreign Missionary Society has secured more than the General Society, and the glory of this has incited others to similar effort; so that it comes to pass that a score of earnest women will visit every member of the church, while there is no agency adequate to that for the work for the General Missionary Society.

Another disturbing element is the constant presence of missionaries at home on furlough or designated to visit the churches soliciting funds for special missions. To a certain degree this is an excellent custom, and guards have been put in operation to prevent loss to the Board by crediting gifts for special purposes to such churches only as have raised the amount apportioned to them for the general work of the Board.

But if money which would naturally have gone to the Society is drawn away from it, every dollar so secured for special gifts affects every other mission. Designated gifts are especially valuable by uniting the giver more closely to the work. Such gifts have frequently been the cause of opening new missions and of stimulating growth in those established, and even preventing the closing of a promising field for want of funds. Properly guarded, with the members of the denomination sufficiently educated to decide wisely, and so devoted to Missions as a whole as to judge with the heart as well as the head, they are to be recognized as most useful. But positive knowledge of the evils suggested demands a reference to them in connection with this phase of the subject.

Another unfavorable element is that of religious denominations undertaking to till a field disproportionate to their resources, or to establish new missions when those already in operation are inadequately supported. It has repeatedly happened that a zealous but ill-informed philanthropist proposed a mission a thousand miles from another of the same denomination, and offered to give a considerable sum to establish it; great enthusiasm has been aroused, and a new mission begun in a part of the world where results could not positively be expected for many years. As a result the Church must consider whether to close the mission or divert moneys from growing missions for the benefit of a losing venture.

A large proportion of professing Christians still do not recognize their responsibility for the conversion of the world. Many churches and many ministers still maintain an indifferent attitude; a minority of these openly declare that it is the business of the Church to evangelize its own territory before taking any action for "outside peoples." The Abyssinian king, Menelik, who adopted this one-sided reasoning might be excused, but not Christians having access to the Bible and conversant with the history of Christianity. A Swedish missionary who was endeavoring to gain a foothold in Abyssinia was taken before King Menelik, who asked him why he had left his home in Scandinavia to come to Abyssinia. The missionary replied that he had come to convert the Abyssinian Jews. "Are there no Jews in your country?" asked Menelik. The missionary admitted that there were a few. "And in all the countries that you have passed through did you find no Jews or heathen?" Jews and heathen, the missionary admitted, abounded. "Then," said Menelik to his guards, "carry this man beyond the frontier, and let him not return until he has converted all the Jews and heathen who lie between his country and mine."

To some this seems the logic of anti-foreign missions, and they say that Menelik penetrated to the core of the matter. But those who think so have much to learn of the causes of the spread of Christianity.

Had Paul converted to Christianity all the Jews and pagans when the men of Macedonia in the vision cried, "Come over and help us"? And had our Lord made Himself known to all in the regions which he visited before he departed for others, how many hundred years would the British Islands have remained in paganism? How long would it have been before the Irish would have been Christianized had not Saint Patrick left his country to exalt them through his wonderful sermons and singing?

"Go ye into all the world, and preach the gospel to every creature" was the divine injunction. Leaving converts made in one place to propagate the work there while the evangelist or missionary goes farther has been the Gospel principle, and by it Christianity is spread. The Abyssinians are Christians, but their early history would show that had the people who came to bring the Gospel to them waited till all in their own countries and all between their countries and Abyssinia had been

converted, Menelik would be a pagan or a Mohammedan.

The Macedonian cry was promptly responded to
by Paul, and, indeed, all his travels and those of
the other apostles show that they did not attempt
to bring about the conversion of all in the vicinity
where they first began to preach: on the contrary,
when they had established a small church and in-
structed its members, they passed on to other
regions, not merely entering open doors but opening them.   By these means light radiated in all
directions from every center, and in time illumi-
nated whole nations.

Misrepresentations, never ending, of missionary work in foreign lands are made by transient
travelers who, without looking for missions, declare that they have found none; or that they in-
quired diligently and could not discover a converted heathen who was not in the pay of the
missions; or that they attended mission services
and that few were present, making no inquiries
concerning other forms of reaching the people.
Others still, not comprehending the necessity of
what is called the "compound" in China, a section
where all the missionary buildings stand, magnify
the size and number of the buildings, and accuse
the missionaries with despising the natives, to
prove it adducing the fact of their dwelling to-

gether.   Business agents associating with wealthy merchants in non-Christian lands frequently receive from them unfavorable impressions.   Sometimes commercial and diplomatic agents on the ground, whose lives there differ materially from their reputations maintained at home, conceive a malignant animosity to missionaries.   Not a few newspapers in every Christian country with avidity take up such misrepresentations, and often magnify them.

The imprudences of various missionaries, and the occasional grave misconduct of one, adds fuel to the flame of scandal, for it is noticeable that, while the account of the misdemeanor is conspicuously displayed, the discipline of the Church, which comes later, is scarcely ever mentioned.   Those who have made misrepresentations and been exposed rarely acknowledge their error, and when they do so they do not repair the damage, for more have seen the false allegation than will see the recantation; and human nature, with rare exceptions, has a better memory for accusations than for denials.

Various forms of imprudence are sometimes committed that cannot be called immoral.   For example, some missionaries from England went to Cairo, and one was so unwise as to enter a Mohammedan mosque and preach to the natives, which inevitably stirred up trouble. Others employ ridicule, are ill-tempered in controversy, and aggressive.

That the wisest missionaries, in their early experiences, fell into methods which were ineffective and were thrown away, is seen in the admirably frank acknowledgment of Bishop Thoburn at the Convention in Toronto, Canada, in 1902:

I will say one or two things that will surprise you. Do not preach against idolatry. Do not preach against the Mohammedan religion. Never preach against any religion *as a religion*, for you merely shut up the hearts of the people who hear you, without accomplishing any good purpose. I am speaking now from experience, for if I could recall a thousand sermons I have preached, I would gladly do it. Never ridicule the religious practices or ideas of the people; that was not our Master's course in this world. But, on the other hand, take that which is common to all religion.

Do not understand, however, that I think that which is common to all religions is going to save the world. You can always assume, as I have found wherever I have been, that there is a Supreme Being. Nobody ever denies His existence, unless he has been educated into that form of unbelief; and, generally, the people who are atheists at the present time are found in England, or America, or France, or places where they have been educated into that form of belief. Instinctively, if you point to the mountains and the stars and the forests and say, "God made all these," the people will agree with you. But you can put it in such language that they will contradict you. I did not know enough to avoid contradiction in earlier days, but I think for the last twenty years in India I never was contradicted by anyone in public. In earlier days I was rather proud of the fact that I could debate for two hours at a time with learned Hindus or Mohammedans, but in later years when appealing to their hearts, after giving them my message, I would say to them: "This is not my word at all; I am giving you a message from God. While I am doing it His Spirit is making you feel in your hearts that what I say is true; and if there is a man here who does not believe that I have been speaking the truth as God has given it to me, I wish he would speak up and tell me." Never has anyone done it; but if I were to say that Jesus Christ is the Eternal Son of God, or that the Koran was false, there would be a dozen Mohammedans on their feet to contradict me at once. God prepares the way of the people, and when you go among them you should always go as a witness of Jesus Christ. Always tell them that you know Him, that He comes with you, that He sends you. Tell them of His love, of His power to save; tell them of the world to which He will take them when life's journey is over, and make it all practical (World-Wide Evangelization, p. 143).

National politics is still an impediment to the success of Missions. Since Dr. Dennis emphasized this fact at length various illustrations of the truth of his setting forth have been seen, of which the Boxer uprising and their treatment of Christian Missions is the most conspicuous illustration. But it is still true that "mission work has to be carried on frequently in countries which are under the political or commercial control of a foreign government, and in such instances it is occasionally true that there is a serious conflict of interest between the government on the one hand and the aim of Missions on the other."

At the present time such difficulties do not stand out so universally and aggressively as they did twenty years ago, when the labor traffic in Malaysia and the Pacific Islands, and the Kanaka traffic among the Islands of Polynesia for the supply of laborers upon the sugar plantations of Queensland, were factors. They were then little else than an organized system of slavery on a large scale, as was seen in the case of Chinese coolies at Singapore, which is a distributing center for the Malaysian Islands. At that time, too, the trade in intoxicants and firearms in the New Hebrides, the oppressive policy of the Dutch in Java, the rum traffic and slave trade in Africa, and what is called the liquor traffic in India were in full and disgraceful action. In various places the tension has been much alleviated, but such situations are still great obstacles.

One of the most deplorable deterrents to accepting Christianity is the confusion of mind produced by the presentation of so many sects endeavoring to Christianize the same races. For example, the Greek, the Arminian, and Coptic Churches exhibit no respect for the efforts of Presbyterians, Baptists, Congregationalists, Lutherans, Methodists, and the Church of England;

and the High Church party of the Church of England frequently, though by no means always, disparage or ignore the work of other religious bodies.

As a rule, in mission lands Roman Catholics are unqualified opponents of Protestant Missions. They are not content "simply to push their own work side by side with evangelical agencies, but they wage war upon Protestant Missions," and seek to render them unpopular and make it impossible to succeed. One who has had ample opportunity to know, declares that "in many countries they are able to count upon the sympathy, and even the practical aid, of the government, native or foreign; but in other lands, as in China, Japan, and India, they are diligent and active in using every available resource to accomplish their purpose."

BUDDHISM

Certain idiosyncrasies of each race, and one or more of the peculiarities of their ancestral religions, make it difficult to reach the people and to substitute the Christian religion for their own. For example, in Siam the most formidable obstacle which confronts the missionaries grows directly out of Buddhism. The people consider that no matter how bad a man may be, nor how profligate he may have been, he can be absolved by building a temple or by ministering to the priests, and, consequently, they feel no need for Christianity. While the priesthood is entirely supported by the government, priests actually derive their subsistence from the people. The priests have unbounded influence over them. "They go about with their rice-pots, and receive contributions, and so terrorize the people that it is really at the peril of their property and of their lives that they refuse them." G. W. Hamilton, D.D., says that the grandmothers of the country are great obstacles. Many young men who are receiving instruction in mission schools are gradually drawn away from heathen customs and ways of thinking. They learn that there is more for them in the religion of Christ than the priests have to offer. Then they go back to their homes, "encounter the autocrat of the household, the grandmother," and her influence invariably does much to counteract the good which the missionaries try to exert.

CONFUCIANISM

Confucianism is hardly a religion, yet it possesses the minds of hundreds of millions, in whose breasts are the same spiritual capacities as are possessed by others. In every city of China, down to those of a third rank, there are temples dedicated to Confucius, and all, including the emperor, offer him religious homage, although he never claimed supernatural origin.   Scented gums and frankincense, tapers and sandalwood are burned on his altars; fruit, wine, and flowers are placed before a tablet on which is inscribed, "O Confucius, our revered master, let thy spiritual part descend and be pleased with this our respect which we now humbly offer to thee." He taught that "all men should worship the spirits of their ancestors, but to go beyond the circle of one's family and worship even departed great ones was simply flattery and wholly unauthorized; that so far as the worship of heaven is concerned, it should be performed by the emperor alone, but for himself and as the representative of the people; but that all, from the emperor down to the meanest, should observe the worship of their ancestors." So firmly rooted are these teachings in the minds of the Chinese that they can hardly accept precepts from other sources. While the followers of Confucius are not conscious of any lack in his teachings, it has been well said that "it does not make full provision for any one of the permanent elements of religion—dependence, fellowship, and progress."

In Japan the difficulty most often met among the intellectual class is rationalism and materialism. "Their minds are void of all those ideas which cluster around the personality of God." Missionaries declare that the ordinary Japanese will agree to almost everything one says with regard to the Gospel of Jesus Christ; he will admit that it is good and that his country ought to have it, but he has no desire to make a personal application of it to his own heart and life.

The business methods of that country have been frequently criticized, and with reason, but they are improving. A missionary in that field about seven years ago testified that he was talking with a young business man, and said to him that if he were faithful and honest under all circumstances, he would surely be promoted. He replied: "You think so, teacher, but that is not true. Unless I fall in line with the practices of the business house with which I am connected, unless I use bribery under certain circumstances, and do things in accord with the policy of the house, I never can be promoted. There is no hope for me." This, unfortunately, could be paralleled in Christian countries, and whenever the Japanese come in contact with anything of the kind it is natural for them to draw the conclusion that in practical experience Christianity is no better as a religion than their own.

Mohammedanism

Mohammedanism is the most difficult opponent of Christianity and its missions and missionaries. There are many millions more of the followers of

Mohammed than there are Christians in all the Protestant Churches on the earth.

Why is it that they are so unconquerable, so unpersuadable, and so active? There are many elements in their religion and in themselves all building up a type of manhood and of religion unlike any other peoples. But the greatest preserver of their religion is the emphasis placed by the prophet on *prayer*.

The second of the five pillars of practical religion in Islam is prayer. The prophet said to the followers, "Seek help from God with prayer and patience." The five periods of prayer are: (1) from dawn to sunrise; (2) when the sun begins to decline from its meridian; (3) midway between noon and sunset; (4) a few minutes after sunset; (5) and when the night has closed in. There are also three voluntary periods of prayer between nightfall and midnight, which are scrupulously observed by the devout.

The ceremony at the mosque is, indeed, impressive. When the sections of prayer are ended "the worshiper kneels on the ground with his left foot bent under him, and placing his hands on his knees recites with a long and reverent voice the *tahiyah:* 'The adorations of the tongue, and of the body and of almsgiving are all of God. Peace be on thee, O prophet, and may the mercy and blessing of God be with thee.' Then, raising the first finger of the right hand, he gives his 'testimony' in these words: 'I testify that there is no god but God, and that Mohammed is His servant and messenger!' He then devoutly offers the following prayer: 'O Lord God, give us the blessings of this life, and of the life to come! Save us from hell!' Two angels are supposed to stand, one on the right hand and the other on the left, and before the worshiper rises from his knees he gives the salutation of peace, first to the right hand and then to the left, and afterward offers prayers and supplications according to his own special needs."

Hughes, the author of the Dictionary of Islam, writes: "This tedious and prolonged form of worship is with slight variations recited in every mosque of Islam all over the world, from the fretted aisles of San Sophia to the sandy floor of some humble praying place on the Sahara." With the average Mohammedan they are little more than vain repetitions; but, according to Mr. Hughes and to many testimonies, "it is this life of constant prayer which retains its mighty hold on Mohammedan peoples and enables them to defy every attempt of Christianity to convert them." Dean Stanley concerning this "vain repetition" says that the prayers among the Mohammedans are "reduced to a mechanical act as distinct from a mental act, beyond any ritual observances in the West. It resembles the worship of a machine rather than of reasonable beings." "This may be so," says Mr. Hughes, "but my twenty years' constant observance of mosque worship convinced me that it exerts an enormous power over the minds of the people, and is the one restraining influence among those savage and semisavage people who acknowledge Mohammed as the 'messenger' of the living God."

Mohammedanism is to-day Christianity's strongest rival. Prebendary Fox, of London, says:

"There is a Mohammedan university in the world, larger than any Christian university, whose students come from a wider area than those in any college in this Christian land. The University of Al Azhar draws its students from India on the east to the western shores of Africa."

As I stood before the doors of that singular building and saw the hundreds of students going to and fro I felt that among them there must be great numbers of Moslem missionaries, and later discovered that most of them served in that capacity.

Mohammedanism is spreading down the Niger and the Congo, and throughout all Africa, taking the place of the degraded religions of animism or fetishism as any superior must, thus creating a greater obstacle to Christianity.

The Christian world has by no means done its duty to the Mohammedans, except sporadically.

Mohammedans are liable to degenerate, as are Christians, because of bad surroundings, as has been found in India where the caste system is invading Mohammedanism. As a matter of fact, they have been unable to resist the Hindu caste feeling. A Mohammedan, according to his religion, has no right to eat with idol-worshipers; they will share the food with Hindus, but will not partake with Christians. "They tell Christians that the reason they do not eat with us is because we drink liquor and eat swine's flesh. The real reason is that they are influenced by the Hindu caste of the people." This is the testimony of one of the most distinguished missionaries. He also affirmed that it is a hard thing for the high-caste Mohammedan to be a Christian. There was a man who came to a missionary and desired to study Greek, but he did not return again until after some ten years had passed. When he reappeared the missionary said to him, "That is a strange way to study Greek." He replied: "I have been a prisoner ever since. My people learned that I was here, and locked me up, and I have only got out now because the house caught fire."

Another unfavorable element is that Mohammedans are fatalists, and will not easily respond on the ground of personal responsibility.

Besides their great university, Mohammedans have many schools. The ingenuity of its professional advocates when they come in contact with Christians is extraordinary. They have nothing to learn from the Jesuits in the way of sophistry. But the main reason why the Mohammedans who acknowledge the God of the Christians and the God of the Jews, and who, though not accepting the deity of Jesus Christ, regard him as one of the greatest of prophets, are so peculiarly difficult to reach, is the tremendous emphasis the prophet placed on prayer.

The Hindus are on the surface polytheists, and much more easily won than Mohammedans. Beneath their polytheism is, however, a pantheistic basis, and the more intelligent Hindu when the Christian minister tries to show him the incongruity of his bowing down to a snake or an idol, is likely to answer: "Is not God all-pervasive, and if he is, is he not in that stone? If he is, I am not worshiping that object, but God."

Next to the Mohammedans, the Jews are more difficult to convert to Christianity than any other class. For this there are many reasons. Among them is their ancestral pride, the strongest and most enduring in the world. Their physiognomy contributes greatly to their isolation, and places a great burden upon them when they profess Christianity. Their rules of disowning, and of diet, and the rite of circumcision strengthen adherence to their ancient allegiance. For a Jew to become a Christian is to cut himself off from all his relatives, to turn his back upon traditions borne in upon him by influences that have been gathering for thousands of years. An obstinacy has been developed by the centuries of Christian brutality. Neither the Catholic nor the Protestant countries can deny their guilt in this particular. Only the younger nations, and not all of them, can plead not guilty against the charge of persecuting the Jews.

Many years ago the Rev. Seigfried Kristeller, a Jew by birth, but educated in one of our theological seminaries, whose parents had ostracized him for his acceptance of Christianity, intrusted to the writer a pathetic letter to his parents. On arriving near their residence the letter was duly delivered; but the answer was received from his parents to the effect that Seigfried Kristeller was to them "as one dead."

Subtle Dangers in the Christian Churches

One of the most dangerous perils to the whole missionary enterprise is the leaven of the naturalistic theories of the origin of the soul of man and of religion. Such conceptions of the history of religion as are put forth by Professor Nathaniel Schmidt would destroy the power of Christianity to make a single intelligent convert. He maintains that *"all religion has the same origin"*; that *"all religion has a natural origin in the impression made by nature upon man and the sense of obligation"*; that *"all religion is subject to the same laws of development"*; that *"all differences in religion are due to peculiarities of the physical environment, the psychical development, and the social conditions."* He asserts that *"if anything in religion is revealed, all is revealed.* There is, indeed, no objection to the use of the term 'revelation' if by it is meant the gradual unfolding of the truth to man's religious consciousness. But as long as it suggests an invidious and untenable distinction between different forms of religion, or a miraculous communication of truth to man, it is wise to avoid the term." He declares that "there is no ground for supposing that any religion has its origin not so much in the common tendencies of man's religious nature as *in the inspiration, originality, and power of the leaders of Buddhism, Mazdaism, Judaism, Christianity, and Islam."* That "those who think so overestimate the originality of a few great religious leaders, and that it fails to recognize the significance of the individual initiative in all forms of religion." He classes *Moses, Jesus, and Mohammed* together, and affirms that "when the mythical and legendary element is removed and the historic facts are ascertained as nearly as possible, it is seen that these men builded

upon foundations laid by others, and also that other
builders followed them, without whom their work
would have been less permanent. It is then
recognized that their reaction against prevailing
tendencies and traditions was but a stronger impulse in the same direction in which myriads of
other souls had moved, that they were only representatives of that progressive element, that cen-
trifugal force, that tendency to vary from the
type, which, in human history as elsewhere in nature, forms the counterpart and supplement of
the conservative element, the centripetal force, the
tendency to preserve the type."

If such views permeate the minds of missionaries and lecturers on Christianity who visit
those regions, or if they could be infused into the
minds of intelligent Buddhists, Confucianists,
and Mohammedans, all hope of leading men to
Christ would disappear.

The Brahma Somaj and the Arya Somaj are
practically "a struggle or spasm of Hinduism to
free itself from idolatry and polytheism and ab-
sorb the ethics of Christianity without its super-
naturalism." Twenty years ago it was said, "It
is hardly to be expected that the Mohammedan, the
Buddhist, the Brahman, the Confucianist, and
others like them will yield to the supremacy of
the Gospel without many curious and pathetic at-

tempts to build their 'half-way houses to Christianity,' or to invent some compromise between the old and the new."

Too high an estimate can easily be put on the contribution of ethnic religions to the religious thought of the world. The difference between Christianity as taught by Christ and Paul and the ethnic religions is the precise ground upon which Christian Missions rest. Flashes of light appear in the writings that have come down and the traditions which persist; but the Christian religion, in its purity, exhibits a different spirit, consists of different principles, and contains a revelation the validity of which may be made to the mere student more than probable by history and logic, and by experiment may be made certain to the consciousness of the believer. A mission based on the assumption that the proponents are more developed than those to whom they speak must fail.

For Christianity to make concessions to other religions, as if those religions originated in the same way that Christianity originated; to admit that Mohammed, or Buddha, or Confucius, or Zoroaster is in the same rank with Jesus Christ, and to concede that the true prophets of the Jews were not inspired of God, in a manner or to a degree not given to men generally or to the prophets of religions that did not recognize the one true eternal God, would be a fatal error.

The claims of Christianity make it impossible for it to blend with other religions.

Seventeen Distinct Circumstances Favorable to Missions

Notwithstanding the circumstances unfavorable to Missions are many and depressing, the circumstances favorable to Missions are also many, more powerful, and greatly encouraging.

1. Valuable tracts of land in the centers of the nations in which missions are maintained and in many of the interior and remote regions have been purchased, and in India, China, Japan are large churches, book publishing concerns, houses for missionaries, schools, deaconesses, hospitals. The property thus invested amounts in the aggregate to a vast sum. Many of the edifices have been built for future ages, and where earthquakes are common the architectural rules of such countries have been observed.

2. Papers, some of them of superior character, are circulated in the native tongues of the people. Libraries have been formed, and frequently learned missionaries have issued the first books of any kind printed in the language of the people they found when they established their missions. Not only this, but several languages have been

reduced to writing for the first time. While the utility of the publications is obvious, the debt that commerce acknowledges is of marked value in maintaining and increasing the influence of the mission and the missionaries. Wherever the material plants exist there are boards and organizations of faculties.

3. Missions are now established in every part of the world where Christianity does not prevail. Some of these can never succeed and ought never to have been established, but even the least of them may contribute to the idea that Christianity has determined to make itself known to every kindred, tribe, and tongue. Protestants have marched around the world, and to name the countries where are no missions would require but a few seconds.

4. To an extent only to be estimated by a wide traveler has the Bible been translated into the language of the people who have been missioned. It is not only the best book for the promotion of morals and religion, but it is an incalculable help to students of foreign languages. One who wishes to visit for business merely that remote region, Dutch Guiana, will find the Bible in that language; if he is in Fo-kien, China, a Bible in the Amoy dialect is at his service. In Zanzibar, Algeria, Morocco, Mesopotamia, and Turkey one finds an Arabic Bible, and if he chances to be

among the American Indians, he sees the Scriptures in the Arapahoe, Cherokee, Choctaw, Chip-
pewa, Delaware, and the Sioux dialects. If he is
a student of languages he will observe the Basque
in three different dialects. The Eskimos are not
forgotten; they have three versions: Greenland,
Labrador, and Hudson Bay. The consul in Finland has his Finnish Bible to aid him in the
study of the language; and the tourists among the
Highlands of Scotland can obtain it in Gaelic.
There are few Irish or Erse in Ireland, or any-
where else, but those few can procure a Protestant translation of the Bible in that language.
The Laplanders have three versions—to accommo-
date the Lapps of Lapland, the Lapps of Norway,
and the Lapps of Sweden. The Zulu, the Tonga,
the Tibetan, each can read the Bible in his own
tongue; four dialects are offered to Spain, and
three of the Romansch to Switzerland.

5. And yet there is more! General Christian
literature is distributed in various languages—a
complete outfit for the theological student, and all
that is necessary for general education. For example: Albanian literature has been greatly increased by the publications of the British and
Foreign Bible Society and Religious Tract Society. It is known that the alphabet of the Bul-
garian language is substantially the same as that
invented by Bishop Cyril in the ninth century and

now commonly called the Russian alphabet. Since the Crimean War a considerable modern literature has sprung up in Bulgaria. It is universally admitted that to this growth American missionaries have given notable stimulus. Dr. Riggs, of the American Board, and Dr. Long, of the Methodist Episcopal Society, made a translation of the entire Bible. In every country the language has been mastered and missionaries immediately inducted into that prevailing. Certain missionaries in every large station speak the native tongues as intelligently as the natives themselves. Others are able to make themselves understood, and are fluent in colloquial style of public speech; while some of the best are able only to convey their meaning in private conversation, and are not able to deliver extended public addresses.

6. The danger points, mental, physical, and social, in the larger mission fields have been discovered and can be pointed out to neophites. An instance of this was given in what may be called the confession of Bishop James M. Thoburn. Not only he, but many other missionaries that have survived the climate and attacks upon their own persons, are communicating their experiences to newly arrived missionaries, and, like consulting surgeons, are at the service of the younger men when difficulties surround them.

7. A noteworthy fact is that there are now sev-

eral generations of converts in the same family. The earlier missionaries could hardly exhibit to the natives a Christian family, and the converts were not members of a thoroughly ecclesiastical and social organization. Now young people speak of their "grandfathers" and "grandmothers" as having been Christians, and to a certain degree the influence of ancestry is working favorably for the consolidation and influence of the Christian community. The churches erected in the East Indian cities, the societies organized, the enterprise constantly shown, commands alike the respect of the natives and the residents of other countries. The same is true in many cities of China, and in Japan. The latter country has organized "The Methodist Church of Japan," and exerts a profound influence, as do other denominations endowed with energy, tact, and sympathy.

8. The growing respect for Christians in large cities radiates in all directions. It is true that attacks are constantly made upon Missions, but many of those attacks are a direct benefit. It cannot have escaped the notice of reading people that a great number of distinguished men have become vindicators of missionaries and Missions. In some instances that which is alleged against them proves to be in their favor, because it challenges investigation. Valuable experience has been gained

and comes to the aid of every new experiment. Necessarily, in the beginning, mistakes were made, but this history is a kind of negative guide, and the history of successes a positive indicator.

9. While there have been and are liable to be difficulties with governments, the causes of such difficulties are diminishing, and the value of the missions is cordially recognized. For a considerable period Americans believed that the Chinese War, known as the Boxer War, was caused by the missionaries, by their imprudence and their interference. But out of that war grew two benefits to Missions: a demonstration that few Protestant missionaries were culpable, and that the majority had demonstrated themselves to be friends of the Chinese, and had carefully avoided running counter to their laws or prejudices.

10. The fidelity of Chinese converts and their willingness to die for their faith gave convincing proof that they had not become Christians for worldly gain. Scarce one of a large number that were killed, and of an equal number that escaped injury, recanted. The bravery, and the aid given by missionaries to the diplomats when shut up in Peking, elicited expressions not only of gratitude but of the highest respect.

11. Another element that is favorable to Mis-

sions is the diminution of prejudice on the part of the people—prejudice founded upon misunderstanding and misrepresentation. This is rapidly passing away in most countries. It would be folly not to expect it in old countries now made new, such as the Philippines; but much more progress in this direction than could reasonably have been anticipated has taken place there.

12. The relations between the different evangelical churches working in the same fields are rapidly growing more fraternal. Indeed, it is necessary to reflect whether such fraternity may not go too far. The difference between evangelical and nonevangelical is even greater *in spirit* than in doctrine. The disposition to enter regions where churches have already been established and are succeeding is diminishing, except where proselyting is intended.

13. One fact of greatest importance is the relation of colonizing movements of the last century to the spread of Missions. Missions have often preceded governmental colonization, for when the embassies reached the field they found Christian missionaries established. The colonizing process, however, has opened doors which without colonization could hardly have been entered with safety.

14. The marvelous change in the attitude of

various denominations toward Missions cannot be detailed. Among the wonders of the age are the rise of the Young Men's Christian Association, and the various young people's societies, such as the Luther League, the Baptist Union, the Society for Christian Endeavor, the Epworth League, and especially the Volunteer Movement of Young Men, and the societies growing out of it.

15. Professor Reinsch, in his valuable book on World Politics, in the department of "National Imperialism," says: "Coming now to the methods by which national expansion is effected, by which, in other words, entrance is gained to territory not yet appropriated by the great powers, we have to consider, in the first place, the influence of Missions. There is a measure of truth in the saying that the flag follows the missionary, and trade follows the flag, although the favorite example cited in Germany—that of the same British ship taking out missionaries and cheaply manufactured idols—may be slightly tinctured with international pleasantry. . . . As the priority of appearance of a nation on unappropriated soil is of great importance under the doctrine of preoccupation, the emissaries of religion who begin the civilizing process are, under the present exaggerated conditions of competition, most valuable advance pickets of national expansion."

This testimony is not from missionaries, but from the point of view of a master of the new science of world politics.

16. The incidental benefit in developing and refining the mental faculties by training schools established by missionaries wherever they go speaks for itself. No reasoning being educated in them, whether or not he give up his ancestral religion for Christianity, will speak evil of those institutions. In many parts of the Turkish empire, in Egypt, in Bulgaria, and several other parts of the world, I endeavored to converse with intelligent natives who had been educated in missionary schools and colleges but for personal or political reasons had not become avowed Christians; and all lauded missionaries and the schools. Dr. J. H. Barrows, a few years before his death, in an address in the city of New York, said: "When I was in India I visited the native city of Jeypore, where I was honored by a call from the Prime Minister of that state, a very learned man, known for his justice and for his ability. He sat down in the missionary's home where I was, and we talked together about many things, and especially about Shakespeare. I found he knew more about the great dramatist than I did, and I was delighted with his accomplishments and with his spirit. As he was leaving the room he took me by the hand and said, *'Dr. Barrows, all that I*

have and am I owe to my education in Duff College, Calcutta.' "

17. The success of medical missions has frequently had an effect like that of ancient miracles. Hospitals, dispensaries, orphanages, foundling asylums, homes for infants, schools and homes for the blind and deaf mutes, leper hospitals and asylums, and homes for their untainted children, have made, and will continue to make, a profound impression. Incidents known to be true are stronger evidence of a proposition of this kind than argumentation. Jacob Chamberlain, doctor of medicine and of divinity, testifies that more than a third of a century ago he established his hospital and dispensary in India, and that a few months after there came in three Brahman clerks of the government office, which was near by. They came for treatment, obtained their tickets, were prescribed for, and sat down to wait for the distribution of the medicine, for no medicines were given out until after the prayer; but, says the Doctor, "as I knew these young Brahmans to be not their own masters but obliged to be at their office at a given hour, and the room was not yet filled, I said to them: 'I will excuse you from waiting to-day for the religious exercise, as I know that you must be at the government office at the stroke of the clock. You can take your medicines and go.' 'No, sir,' said they, 'if you please we

will wait for the prayer.' I said, 'That is my rule, but I make an exception in your case, because I know you may be in great haste to go.' 'No, sir, we will wait for the reading and the prayer, because after your prayer to your God who sent you here to heal us, we believe that these medicines will have a much greater effect upon us, and though we be not of your religion, we do believe that your prayers are heard, and we will wait for the reading of the Scripture and the prayer.' " A case of a different kind among the Mohammedans is reported by Dr. J. L. Humphrey, a well-known missionary to India: "There is great power in medicine for winning one's way to the hearts and enlisting the sympathy of the people. On one occasion there was a Mohammedan trying to enter into an argument with me who used some very discourteous words. He came to me a little while after and apologized, saying: 'I did not know that you were a doctor; I did not know that you had charge of the hospital over there. I do not wish to offend you, as I may be sick to-morrow and want you; I want you to be my friend, so I beg your pardon.' "

The conclusion drawn from this comparison of things unfavorable and favorable to the success of Missions is, that after giving every value to every favorable and unfavorable element, and adding the spirit and letter of the Christian religion, and to

that the Providence of God, and His will that all
nations shall hear the Gospel, and to that that the
spirit of Missions at home and abroad is essential for the maintenance of Christianity upon the
earth, there can be no doubt that the Gospel of
Jesus Christ (though it may be delayed longer
than the overenthusiastic think) will become the
dominant religion in all the earth.

THE FOURTH LECTURE

WHAT OF THE PRESENT AND THE FUTURE OF FOREIGN MISSIONS?

THE FOURTH LECTURE

WHAT OF THE PRESENT AND THE FUTURE OF FOREIGN MISSIONS?

ACCORDING to a reliable tabulated statement there are in existence one hundred and eighty Protestant foreign missionary organizations. The table includes denominational boards of missions, corporations, and private societies.

There are twenty-eight societies working for the Christianization of the Jews. Direct missions to them have not usually been successful; but a slowly increasing number may be found in various local congregations of different Christian Churches.

Roman Catholic missions are found everywhere, and the number of religious orders and societies engaged in that work is amazing. Of the orders there are more than fifty; and all the missionary priests have auxiliaries in communities of brotherhoods and sisterhoods.

PROTESTANT MISSIONS IN ROMAN CATHOLIC COUNTRIES

The question is frequently asked, Why do Protestants send missionaries to Roman Catholic countries? The answer is, that in some Roman

Catholic countries a large proportion of the people, though Roman Catholic in name, are not Christian in spirit or practice; also there are in so-called Catholic countries great numbers of infidels and agnostics. Such Protestants as send missionaries to countries where Roman Catholics preponderate do so that there may be a presentation of Christianity so different from that made by the Church of Rome as to uproot particular doctrines, sacraments, or ceremonies believed by Protestants to have been inventions. They wish to show that true Christianity is *not* loaded with the numerous and burdensome tenets, customs, and exactions which have accumulated through the ages in the Roman Catholic Church, especially with respect to the relations of Church and State. They are chiefly education, freedom of conscience, speech, and the press; the infallibility of the Pope, the sacerdotal powers of the priests, the undue homage to deceased saints and the Virgin Mary, prayers for the dead, Purgatory, the confessional, indulgences, enforced celibacy upon priests and nuns, the belief that the substance of the wine and bread in the holy communion is transmuted into the literal substance of the body and blood of Christ, and the consequent elevation and worship of the Host; the withholding of the wine from communicants except to the priest celebrating the mass, the refusal of divorce, even for adultery, and other unscriptural

Another question of much delicacy and difficulty has arisen. Shall Protestants of one Communion send missionaries to countries ecclesiastically and civilly under the influence of another orthodox denomination? The Methodist Episcopal and the Baptist Churches are involved in this on a larger scale than any other. Missions in Germany, Sweden, Norway, Denmark, and Finland, Russia, are sustained by both Baptists and Methodists.

The answer is this: Those missions originated in the following manner: natives of those countries emigrated to this country in great numbers. The Protestant bodies dominating in the Fatherland did not exist in a large part of the United States, and where they did they were not adequate to gather in the constant stream of immigrants, and when and where they could, many went astray. Many of these were converted in Methodist and Baptist revivals. They wrote home, detailing their vivid experiences. Then, in many instances, relatives sought and found similar experiences. Many returned from America, either to reside permanently or on visits. Small companies gathered to hear of their new and enthusiastic news and feelings.

In all these countries the people of the State Churches are divided into three classes of unequal numbers: one rationalistic, another thoroughly evangelistic, another simply conforming more or less to the ancestral ceremonies.

Among the evangelistics there were many who could not endure the little companies, nor what seemed to them the extravagances of the converts. This lack of sympathy, together with ridicule from the rationalists, at first, caused the converts to ask Methodists in America to send over preachers. This was the almost accidental way in which the missions were originated not only in Germany but in Scandinavian countries.

It is the opinion of many devout Lutherans that the advent of Methodism has been a benefit to evangelical Christianity. Already the third generation of German and Scandinavian Methodists are on the scene, reciprocal with those Conferences in the United States which are conducted in the languages of their fathers.

There is no desire to see the true Churches of Christ disturbed or preyed upon by Methodists, and those who are in the spirit of the Gospel, and demonstrate it by the works, will not be disturbed.

VALUE OF CORRECT MISSIONARY STATISTICS

An acquaintance with statistics is of immense value as showing that every denomination in the world is interested in foreign missions, except some small sects which exhibit other indications of fanaticism, such as the "Old Two-

Seed-in-the-Spirit" Presbyterian, Baptists, and
others who also in addition to missionary societies,
regard with marked disfavor other "modern institutions," such as Sunday schools and theological seminaries, and some small offshoots from
Methodism, Presbyterianism, etc.

GRANDEUR OF FOREIGN MISSIONS

It might be said without fear of material contradiction that the only enterprise in which all
Protestants, Roman Catholics, Orthodox Greek,
and Russo-Greek Churches agree is Missions.
Comprehension of their grandeur is clarified and
deepened by considering the era when modern
foreign Protestant Missions may be said to have
originated, which dates from William Carey's
ringing call.

Carey was born in 1761, and at the age of
twenty-five entered the Baptist ministry. He
soon became impressed with the idea of a mission
to the heathen, frequently conversing with ministers, to whom he attempted to demonstrate its
practicability and importance. At an early age he
"devoured books, especially of science, history,
voyages," and in spite of scanty advantages mastered Latin, Greek, Hebrew, Dutch, and French.
None of his brethren sympathized in his constant
theme—a mission to the heathen. Early in his
pastoral career he published a work entitled An

Inquiry into the Obligation of Christians to Use Means for the Conversion of the Heathen. Within six years the seed which he had been diligently sowing produced a plentiful harvest. At a meeting of the Ministers' Association at Nottingham, May 31, 1792, he preached from this text, "Enlarge the place of thy tent." He laid down two propositions: "Expect great things from God," and "Attempt great things for God." By this discourse he conquered the Ministers' Association, and in about six months the English Baptist Missionary Society was formed. Carey at first was strongly inclined to go to Africa, but offered to go wherever the Society might send him, and India was selected.

He embarked on an English vessel, but, on account of objections made against missionaries by the East India Company, the commander of the ship was forbidden to take him or his friend, John Thomas, a surgeon, and they were debarked. Carey, however, with undaunted courage, sailed in a Danish vessel, and landed unobserved in India.

In the same year that Carey began missionary work in India the Society for the Propagation of the Gospel opened a mission in *New South Wales.* The next was established by the London Missionary Society in the island of *Tahiti.* Prior to that the same Society had begun missions in *South Africa,* and in *India,* at Calcutta. Next appears on the scene the Church Missionary Society, which opened a mission in *West Africa.* The Baptist Missionary Society (Carey's) planted one in *Ceylon.* Then the London Missionary Society began work at *Hongkong.* A year later the Dutch appeared with a mission in *Java;* the Church Missionary Society in the *West Indies;* and, for the first time in its history, the American Board of Commissioners for Foreign Missions appeared in *Bombay;* and the American Baptist Union carried the Gospel to *Burma.*

In 1814 the Wesleyan Methodist Missionary Society selected *South America* as the site of its first regular mission; the Church Missionary Society added to its list *New Zealand* and *Ceylon,* and, speedily, the *Levant.* The London Missionary Society now entered *Malta.*

India appears to have been the chief center of Missions, for in 1816 the General Baptist Society, now the Baptist Missionary Society, sent a missionary to *Bengal,* and the American Board one to *Ceylon.* They were followed, in 1817, by the Wesleyan Methodist Society, which flung out its banner in *Bengal.* In 1818 the Church Missionary Society planted itself in *Ceylon,* and the or extra-scriptural doctrines and customs imposed upon its devotees. Furthermore, they conceive that the introduction of Protestantism into Catholic countries contributes to the spreading of principles of human equality, as the freedom of conscience, of speech, and of the Press, and non-denominational Education at the public expense, and creates in time a degree of influence which will affect favorably the Catholic Church as a whole, as has already been proved in American Catholicism. No traveler in Spain, France, Italy, Portugal, and South and Central America, Cuba, and the Philippines can fail to perceive a marked difference between the Roman Catholic peoples there, and those of that faith long domiciled in the United States and Great Britain.

Nevertheless, the transformation of pagans, Mohammedans, and Buddhists into Roman Catholics is a definite advance, and the present progress of Roman Catholics in such lands is to be considered a gain to general Christianity. This is acknowledged by those who cannot accept the claims of the Papacy to universal dominion, the validity of the added five sacraments, or believe it wise to appropriate public money for the support of sectarian schools, or allow teachers in schools supported by public funds, to instruct the children in Romish forms of religion, either by book, speech, or the wearing of ecclesiastical vestments.

London Missionary Society opened the mission in *Madagascar.*

In 1819 the American Board appeared in *Syria* and in the *Hawaiian Islands;* and the Church Missionary Society in *Egypt.*

The Society for the Propagation of the Gospel opened in *Cape Colony* in 1820, and the next year in *Calcutta.*

In 1821 the Scottish Missionary Society, afterward the United Free Church of Scotland, added its strength to the *Zulu* mission work; the American Baptist Missionary Union started a mission in the new republic of *Liberia.* In 1822 the United Free Presbyterian Church of Scotland organized one in *Calcutta,* and the Wesleyan Methodist Society inaugurated one in *New Zealand.*

In 1828 the American Board entered *Greece,* and the London Missionary Society entered *Siam.* The first to settle in *Persia* was the Basel Society; and the first to visit *Canton* the American Board, in 1830, the same year that the Church Missionary Society appeared in *Abyssinia* and the Protestant Episcopal Church in *Greece.*

The year 1831 is notable for the beginning of the work of the American Board in *Constantinople.* That enterprising body, also, in 1833, entered *China* through Bangkok. The Board of Foreign Missions of the Presbyterian Church in the United States then organized its first mission

in the *Northwest Provinces of India.* The same
year the American Board entered *Persia,* and the
Methodist Episcopal Church invaded *Liberia.*

In 1835 three missions were established, one by
the Protestant Episcopal Church, in *Shanghai,*
one by the Free-will Baptists, in *India,* and the
third by the Presbyterian Board, in *Liberia.*

In 1836 *Borneo* was the first foreign mission
of the Reformed Church in America; and the
Methodist Episcopal Church in *South America.*

The Presbyterian Board set up in 1838 its banner in *Malaysia;* in 1839 the London Missionary
Society entered *New Hebrides.* The Lutheran
Missionary Society of the United States began
mission work in the *Central Provinces of India* in
1840. In 1841 the Foreign Missionary Society of
the Presbyterian Church in Ireland entered *India;*
also the Welsh Calvinistic Mission raised its
standard in *North India.*

In 1844 the South American Missionary Society opened a mission in *Tierra del Fuego.* In
1852 the American Board entered *Micronesia.* In
1854 the United Presbyterian Church commenced
in Egypt, where their success has been remarkable.
In 1857 the Methodist Episcopal Church set up
a mission in *Bulgaria.* The next year the American Board entered that country, but not in the regions occupied by the Methodists.

Not till 1859 in the catalogue of Missions does

the name now known and respected (and in a sense feared) by the whole world appear—*Japan.* In that year the Protestant Episcopal Church, the Reformed Church in America, and the Presbyterian Church entered *Japan.* In 1865 foreign missions of the Presbyterian Church in England entered *Japan,* and in the same year *Formosa,* now practically a part of Japan. In 1869 the American Board entered *Japan;* also the Church Missionary Society, and in 1871 the Methodist Church of Canada and the Woman's Union Missionary Society followed. In 1872 the Methodist Episcopal Church and the American Baptist Missionary Union established missions there, as did, in 1873, the Society for the Propagation of the Gospel; in 1876, the Evangelical Association; in 1877, the Cumberland Presbyterian Missionary Society; in 1879, the Reformed German; in 1880, the Methodist Protestant Church Missionary Society; in 1883, the Disciples; in 1885, the Presbyterian Church, South; the American Friends' Board of Foreign Missions, the German Evangelical Synod of the United States, and Board of Missions of the Methodist Episcopal Church, South; in 1888, the Christian Mission, commonly called Brethren; in 1890, the Southern Baptist Convention, and the Universalist Church; in 1892, the Evangelical Lutheran General Council Missions; also the Canadian Church of England; in 1893, a Mission to Lepers, the United Brethren in Christ, and the United Methodist Free Churches of England, Home and Foreign Missions.

This seems a remarkable fulfillment of the words, "He that hath, to him shall be given."

In 1861 the Protestant Episcopal Church entered *Haiti,* and the London Missionary Society *New Guinea.*

Mexico was entered in 1870 by the Protestant Episcopal Church; by the Methodist Episcopal Church in 1872; and by the Methodist Episcopal Church, South, in the same year.

In 1874 the Swedish National Missionary Society entered the *Congo Free State.*

In 1884 the Presbyterian Church entered *Korea;* and in 1885, the Methodist Episcopal Church.

In 1886 the Archbishop's Mission entered *Persia,* creating considerable friction, as that country had already several missions, and *Arabia* was entered at Aden, by the United Free Church of Scotland.

In 1888 the Cumberland Presbyterian Missionary Society entered *Mexico.* In 1889 the Methodist Episcopal Church entered *Malaysia.*

The *Philippines* were entered by the Presbyterians in 1899; also the American Baptist Union, the Methodist Episcopal Church, the Church

Mission, the Seventh Day Adventists; and in 1901
United Brethren in Christ, and in 1902 the
American Board of Commissioners for Foreign
Missions.

In 1899 the Presbyterian Board, the Southern
Presbyterian Board, the American Missionary
Association, the Foreign Christian Missionary
Society, Disciples, the Evangelical Lutheran Gen-
eral Council, and the Methodist Episcopal
Church, entered *Porto Rico.*

STRIKING CONTRASTS

Half a century ago Russia and Japan, seven
thousand miles apart, and farther by water, could
never have come together in great armies; but so
amazing has been scientific achievement that the
late war was waged in a region which one army
could reach in four days, and the other in four
weeks; and throughout the entire war the rest of
the world received daily information from the field.

Commodore Perry in 1854—when a few
wooden vessels made the long journey to Japan—
found a people who had on its statute books: "So
long as the sun shall continue to warm the earth,
let no Christian be so bold as to come to Japan;
and let all know that the king of Spain himself,
or the Christian's God, or the Great God of all,
if he dare violate this command, shall pay for it
with his head."

Fifty-four years ago a director of the East India Company declared that he would rather see "a band of devils in India than a band of missionaries."

When The Christian Advocate published the editorial which elicited sufficient contributions from readers to justify the opening of a Methodist Episcopal Mission in Korea, it had not been three years since Korea was called the "Hermit Nation."

The Rev. Dr. Cuyler, ever both concise and vivid, stated that in the year 1800 no steamer plowed the waters, no locomotive traversed an inch of soil, no photographic plate had ever been kissed by the sunlight, no telephone had ever talked from town to town, steam had never driven mighty mills, and electric currents had never been harnessed into telegraph and trolley wires.

The address of the Bishops of the Methodist Episcopal Church in 1900, written by the late Bishop Andrews, says of the beginnings of that denomination:

In all the land there was no power loom, no power press, no large manufactory in textiles, wood or iron, no canal. The possibilities of electricity and light, heat, and power were unknown and unsuspected. The cotton gin had just begun its revolutionary work. Intercommunication was difficult, the postal service slow and costly, literature scanty and of inferior quality.

When, in 1847, the first Methodist missionaries went to China the voyage required nearly one hundred and twenty days.

Dr. Calvin Mateer, who was six months in 1863 in reaching Chefoo, China, returned in 1902 in a comfortable journey of one month. Stanley "could now go from Glasgow to Stanley Falls, in Africa, in forty-three days," and to-day railway trains run constantly between Saint Petersburg and Peking.

Dr. Brown, in New Forces in Old China, recounts an experience pertinent to this: "Camping one night in Far Northern Laos after a toilsome ride on elephants, I realized that I was 12,000 miles from home, at as remote a point almost as it would be possible for man to reach. All about was wilderness relieved only by the few houses of a small village. But, walking into that tiny hamlet, I found at the police station a telephone connecting with the telegraph office at Chieng-Mai, so that although I was on the other side of the planet I could have sent a telegram to my New York office in a few minutes."

Of the innumerable contrasts I emphasize the following: Nearly all countries were closed to foreigners one hundred years ago; missions were abhorred, and at home were far from popular. As late as 1808 the celebrated Sydney Smith ridiculed Carey in an article in the Edinburgh Review, of which he was one of the chief lights, as the "consecrated cobbler" and "maniac."

General Lane, the first territorial governor of Oregon, desiring to reach his post, started from his home in Indiana August 27, 1848, traveling overland to San Francisco, and thence by water, the journey occupying six months.

The modes of travel, with respect to speed, comfort and time, have revolutionized the postal communications of the world.

When our missionaries in China went to the interior they could get letters only by the aid of couriers or chance travelers. Now the modern system, introduced by Sir Robert Hart, already includes five hundred of the principal cities of the empire. Mails can be received from all parts of Europe in two or three weeks. Missionaries in India, Japan, and China can keep continuously informed.

When, two decades ago, the Revised Version of the New Testament was issued a Chicago paper received it by telegraph and distributed it to the public the next morning.

As Dr. Arthur Brown, secretary of the Presbyterian Board of Foreign Missions, rose to address a meeting of the English-speaking residents of Canton, China, in September, 1901, a message on the very day of the event was handed him, which read,

"President McKinley is dead." And what shall be said of the eighteen hundred submarine cables of over two hundred thousand miles? To this must be added wireless telegraphy in every direction that needs no cable, that sends out countless messages when it sends one. The story of the Republic, and the rescue of every soul on board, speaks more eloquently of these marvelously changed conditions than the tongue of any orator.

Sixty years ago it was hardly safe, in most parts of the world outside of Europe, for a traveler, without armed attendants, to go very far from the cities containing Legations from other nations.

In 1863 I was preaching in Plymouth Church, Brooklyn, Mr. Beecher being in Europe pleading for the Federal Government, then imperiled by the Civil War. A member of the family which entertained me interested me greatly. She was advanced in years, and somewhat shattered nervously. Her appearance indicated refinement, and traces of unusual beauty remained. At the dinner table she made singular motions; apparently her thoughts were far away, and her expression was that of one perceiving mentally some dreadful scene. There was nothing that suggested impaired reason, and for the greater part of the time she listened to the conversation. After she

had retired one of her daughters told me that her
father was the captain of a large sailing vessel
carrying goods to Oriental ports; that her mother
sometimes accompanied him on his long voyages;
that the ship had been wrecked on the coast of
China, and her mother was taken captive, placed
in a cage, was carried through different parts of
the great empire for several months as a part of
a show, and that over the cage was the inscription
in Chinese, "A Real Live American Woman."
Alone, and unable to communicate with any
American, and never seeing one who spoke English
in the motley crowds that stared at her, the poor
woman barely survived each horrid day. When
she was too ill to rise at the command of the show-
man, a long pole was thrust at her as one might
rouse a sleepy lion for the entertainment of children visiting a menagerie. When she was almost
at death's door a consul of one of the European
states, who could read Chinese, saw the inscription and hastened to her rescue. He secured her
release; but she never fully recovered her nervous
tone, and often when conversing with friends, for
a moment she had this dreadful vision—the crowd
grimacing and hurling anathemas at her. This
story, as graphically told as one of the parables in
the New Testament, burned its way into the
chambers of memory. Not being able to give
it absolute credence, when Mr. Beecher returned

from Europe I repeated it to him, and he assured me that the amazing account was absolutely true.

Could such a protracted outrage occur to-day wherever missionaries have penetrated, or in any place where the authorities know of danger to or cruel treatment of a European or American citizen?

The respect of all non-Christian countries for Missions has been augmented incalculably. It is now comparatively safe for missionaries to explore any country. When the first Europeans went to China and saw the Chinese maps, they found that the Celestial Empire took up the greater part of the map, and in the corners was a writing which, translated, read, "Unknown Territories Inhabited by Barbarians."

One hundred years ago if one had prophesied that all the great Powers and many smaller would undertake to colonize, none would have believed it. But every effort at colonization opens new doors for Missions.

Respect at home for missionaries has quadrupled in the past half century, and that respect does not depend upon transient action or reaction, but upon the quality of the work and the character of the missionaries. The success much resembles the evolution of nations from small settlements. These began with decades or centuries of hardships, obscurity, discouragements, and isolation; then a gradual growth was seen, and this finally advanced by leaps and bounds. Some missions are now in the first stage, others in the second, and an increasing number in the third. Settlements have sprung up like Jonah's gourd. A few have had almost as brief a life. Others have flourished and even outstripped those surely advancing. Of these the most conspicuous in the whole history of Missions is Korea.

Medical missions first opened Korea to the message, but at that time the preaching of the Gospel was forbidden. No meetings for religious worship could be held elsewhere than on mission compounds; then the services had to be conducted quietly, and baptism had to be administered in secret. The first year after the medical work began, which was in 1884, there was a fearful cholera epidemic, and the lay missionaries, led by physicians and nurses, worked day and night for weeks in the fight with that disease. The Korean people wondered at this, but still more were they astonished by the conduct and bearing of the Korean Christians. It is impossible to state definitely how many Christian converts are there, and to supply the needed preachers and teachers. The Koreans build their own chapels, support their own evangelists and nearly all their own school teachers.

MISSIONARY LEADERS

No important result has ever been accomplished by one man working entirely alone, nor was ever a grand and permanent work done by the multitude without leaders. Leaders are of various types. Some conceive great plans, which other men bring to perfection and popularize. Many are better qualified to work a plan than to plan their work. As foreign missions are almost all-inclusive in their needs and methods, every type of leadership appears there. One type operates so quietly as to escape observation, and not until he has been removed from the place of responsibility, or finished his career upon the earth, is his leadership adequately estimated or gratefully acknowledged.

GEORGE DANA BOARDMAN belongs to the latter type. Although but thirty years of age, and but three years in the service, his willing sacrifice gave a hero whose fame will endure forever to the Baptist Board of Missions. Just before sunset on the last day of his life, he was carried from his bed to the water side, and in his presence his colleague baptized thirty-four Karens. Though very ill, when advised to turn aside for rest, he answered, "The cause of God is more important than my life, and if I return now our whole object will be defeated."

DAVID BRAINERD was another who led by his influence and life. He was a missionary to the Indians, and was not remarkable for learning, but before his early death he accomplished wonderful and widespread results. It was his journals, published after his death, that made JONATHAN EDWARDS a missionary to the Indians of Stockbridge. To him, also, HENRY MARTIN traced his decision to become a missionary; and even WILLIAM CAREY was indebted for much of the inspiration which had shaped his decision.

Of very different type indeed was WILLIAM BUTLER, the founder of the India Mission of the Methodist Episcopal Church, and who also founded the mission of the same Church in Mexico. William Butler went through the Sepoy Rebellion, a price upon his head. After twenty-six years he returned to India, and at Bareilly, where the first meeting of his mission had been held, gave thanks to God for its growth and power during the years that had intervened.

DR. TITUS COAN was the chief evangelist of the Hawaiian Islands, and his career filled with enthusiasm all lovers of Christianity. He preached forty-three times in eight days, made tours through the island, and had the joy of seeing thousands become genuine and intelligent Christians.

It may be said of ALEXANDER DUFF that he led the world in Missions by pen, voice, and example.

THOMAS COKE established missions in Nova Scotia and in the West Indies, superintended the work on the West India Islands, and finally turned his attention to Ceylon and India. He was so anxious to commence this mission that he offered to defray all the expenses, amounting to six thousand pounds. As he was then advanced in years his friends tried to dissuade him from the long voyage, but he said, "If you will not let me go, you will break my heart." He, however, did not reach India, but died suddenly in his cabin, and was buried at sea. His spiritual leadership continued long after he was dead, and he had more to do in stirring up missionary spirit in the newly formed Methodist Episcopal Church than any other of its earliest supporters.

CYRUS HAMLIN was the man of all work of the American Board, and made that body known throughout the world during the Crimean War, and again by establishing Robert College. To write his biography would be a pleasure, on the principle that the greater the number of unusual incidents in the subject's career the more interesting the story of his life to author and reader.

ADONIRAM JUDSON in the thirty-seven years of his missionary service was conspicuous for thorough work, fervent piety, powerful intellect, adaptation to every position, and especially by suffering for the cause of God. He was thrown into the death-prison during the war between England and Burma, and there lay bound with five pairs of fetters for seventeen months. In that trial of faith he manifested the same determination which had sustained him when, after going out as one of the early missionaries of the American Board as a Congregationalist, he conscientiously changed his views, and, withdrawing, became a Baptist.

ROBERT MOFFAT was a man of stimulating type. He spent his missionary life in Africa, and for years he labored preaching and teaching without witnessing conversions; but after he had completed a translation of Saint Luke, and in order to publish it had learned the printer's art, the mission became prosperous. Unaided, he completed the translation of the whole Bible into Bechuana. His life is thus summed up by one of his biographers: "On entering the missionary work he found the people murderous savages; when he died he left them with a written language of their own, enabling them to appreciate and cultivate the habits of civilized life."

DAVID LIVINGSTONE stands in the front rank of explorers and missionaries. When urged by Sir Roderick Murchison to relinquish the missionary work and devote himself only to discovery, he wrote: "I would not consent to go simply as a geographer, but as a missionary and do geography by the way." Twice was he lost and found, the second rescue making an immortal reputation for Stanley, who discovered and brought him back to civilization five days after he had written, in his extremity, "I commit myself to the Almighty Disposer of Events."

The McAll Mission, though undenominational, shows its founder, the Rev. ROBERT W. McALL, to be a true missionary leader. In France, Corsica, Tunis, and Algiers he did not aim at anything except purely evangelistic teaching. In France he did not attempt to win converts from the Catholic Church, though many French Catholics who did not withdraw became evangelical in spirit. Most of his early converts were made from those who had shaken off their early Roman Catholic views and had become atheistic.

The MORAVIANS, in view of their small numbers, surpass the world in mission work; their system befits their situation, and they abound with leaders who lead.

ROBERT MORRISON was the founder of Protestant Missions in China. His name will never be forgotten. He was a translator, and to show his determination and adherence he writes, "I have been twenty-five years in China, and am now beginning to see the work prosper."

JOHN STRONACH was a man of no common order. He made a brilliant record by the translation of the Bible into Chinese. He was "a most idiomatic master of Chinese," and it is said that it was a charm to hear him speak. Dr. Stronach was the author of a pamphlet containing a masterly setting forth of the difficulties felt by a literary Chinaman, and the answers to them by the missionary. He was successful as an evangelist, and labored indefatigably in starting stations. "With all this he was overflowing with high spirits, and had an unfailing fund of humor, which served him well in conflicts with opponents who became troublesome."

WILLIAM TAYLOR was probably the most successful world-covering evangelist who ever lived. He was his own society and secretary, and therefore did not receive attention from encyclopedists; but, speaking through interpreters, he was at home in any part of the world. He established many missions on the "Pauline principle," as he termed it, of living upon the indigenous resources of the country wherever he planted a mission. None ever visited Australia as an evangelist whose work there endured as did his. In India and in South America his name will ever be revered.

The foregoing are types of leaders in the field. "Time would fail me" to speak of the lay leaders and secretaries whose eloquence and industry have conserved the interests of the missionary societies and aroused the people to a sense of obligation and opportunity.

THE GIFT OF MISSIONS TO ANTHROPOLOGY

Foreign missions have added immensely to the world's knowledge, not only upon cosmopolitan questions but upon man. In every race with which foreign missions have dealt, however low, ignorant, or fierce, some of the natives have shown a capacity for applying themselves to the acquisition of learning. They have demonstrated the truth of the apostle's statement that "God hath made of one blood all nations of men for to dwell on all the face of the earth, and hath determined the times before appointed, and the bounds of their habitation."

This fact could be supported by competent testimony from many lands and different races, but the only instance which I will adduce relates to the improvement of natives of the South Sea Islands, and my witness shall be a man who shares with Tennyson, Holmes, and Abraham Lincoln a place among the distinguished men born in 1809—Charles Darwin, who would by many be considered the last man to have definite connection with Christian Missions.

In 1870 he wrote to B. J. Sullivan a letter in which he said:

I had never heard a word about the success of the Tierra del Fuego mission. It is most wonderful, and shames me, as I always prophesied utter failure. It is a grand success. I shall feel proud if your committee think fit to elect me an honorary member of your Society.

The Archbishop of Canterbury, speaking at the annual meeting of the South American Missionary Society, said that the Society "drew the attention of Charles Darwin, and made him, in his pursuit of the wonders of the kingdom of nature, *realize that there was another kingdom as wonderful and more lasting.*" The Archbishop in making that statement went too far, and Mr. Darwin's son and biographer sets the matter right. There being in the Daily News, of London, for four successive days in 1885, some discussion of this subject, Admiral Sir James Sullivan, a lieutenant on board the Beagle with Darwin, wrote to that paper a "clear account" of Darwin's connection with the Society.

This is the Admiral's letter:

Your article in the Daily News of yesterday induces me to give you a correct statement of the connection between the South American Missionary Society and Mr. Charles Darwin, my old friend and shipmate for five years. I have been closely connected with the Society from the time of Captain Allen Gardiner's death, and Mr. Darwin has often expressed to me his conviction that it was utterly useless to send missionaries to such a set of savages as the Fuegians, probably the very lowest of the human race. I had always replied that I did not believe any human beings existed too low to comprehend the simple message of the Gospel of Christ. After many years, I think about 1869, but I cannot find the letter, he wrote to me that the recent accounts of the mission proved to him that he had been wrong and I right in our estimates of the native character, and the possibility of doing them good through missionaries; and he requested me to forward to the Society an inclosed cheque for five pounds, as a testimony of the interest he took in their good work. On June 6th, 1874, he wrote: "I am very glad to hear so good an account of the Fuegians, and it is wonderful." On June 10th, 1879: "The progress of the Fuegians is wonderful, and had it not occurred would have been to me quite incredible." On January 3d, 1880: "Your extracts about the Fuegians are extremely curious, and have interested me much. I have often said that the progress of Japan was the greatest wonder in the world, but I declare that the progress of Fuegia is almost equally wonderful." On March 20th, 1881: "The account of the Fuegians interested not only me but all my family. It is truly wonderful what you have heard from Mr. Bridges about their honesty and their lan-

guage. I certainly should have predicted that not all
the missionaries in the world could have done what has
been done." On December 1st, 1881, sending me his
annual subscription to the Orphanage at the Mission
Station, he wrote: "Judging from the Missionary Jour-
nal, the mission in Tierra del Fuego seems going on
quite wonderfully well" (Vol. II, p. 308, Life and Letters of Charles Darwin, published in this country).

I adduce the foregoing simply in proof that
those apparently undeveloped savages were capable
not merely by a slow process of successive generations, but in one generation, and under the influence of missionaries, of such improvement as
astonished Christians and Charles Darwin.

What of the Future?

In the year 1907 there were 18,591 Protestant
foreign missionaries in non-Christian lands, and
the Christians of Europe and America gave that
year for their support and for churches, schools,
hospitals, printing presses, and other work under
their care, $21,280,147. The stations and out-
stations occupied aggregate 36,748. The number
of definitely known adult converts and adherents
is already 6,202,631, and it is rapidly increasing.[1]

---

[1] The World Atlas of Christian Missions, published by the Student
Volunteer Movement for Foreign Missions in 1911, and based on the
Statistical Atlas presented at the World Missionary Conference at Edinburgh in 1910, but enlarged to include missions in Roman Catholic
lands (except in Europe), gives the total of foreign missionaries as
21,307; stations and out-stations, 38,557; total of Christian adherents,
6,837,736. The Missionary Review of the World for January, 1911,
gives the income of the Protestant missionary societies of the world
for 1910 as $26,890,104.

Have missions done all that could have been rationally and spiritually expected of them?

Who can tell? But with the present appliances in ten years this showing should be doubled.

In the course of human development doubtless some existing religions will dissolve; some new religions will be born and die, and some will have a longer lease of life.

Before the world is Christianized the great non-Christian religions must be modified almost beyond recollection or entirely disappear.

Those who think this epoch to be near I cannot understand. Those who prophesied fifty years ago that in less than thirty years the whole world would be evangelized have failed. And those who from the time of His ascension have declared the coming of the Lord to be near, have succeeded each other without the longed-for vision.

During a few decades last past great success has attended the labors of genuine missionaries and missions; and changes in favor of the spread of Christianity have followed speedily.

The CHURCH must sow the seed; the MASTER must give the rain, the light and heat, till the harvest time of the world.